# An Impossible *Dream*

*Reagan, Gorbachev, and*
*a World Without the Bomb*

Guillaume Serina

*Translated from the French by David A. Andelman*

Introduction by Mikhail Gorbachev
Afterword by David A. Andelman

PEGASUS BOOKS

NEW YORK LONDON

AN IMPOSSIBLE DREAM

Pegasus Books Ltd.
148 W 37th Street, 13th Floor
New York, NY 10018

First Pegasus Books edition July 2019

Interior design by Maria Fernandez

Library of Congress Cataloging-in-Publication Data is available.

ISBN: 978-1-64313-084-2

10 9 8 7 6 5 4 3 2 1

Printed in the United States of America
Distributed by W. W. Norton & Company, Inc.
www.pegasusbooks.us

*To Benjamin and Daniel*

# Contents

# Introduction

## by Mikhail Gorbachev

Thirty years after the Reykjavík summit, has the world learned the most fundamental lesson we sought to convey at this summit of the world's two superpowers?

Today's relationship between Russia and America is strained. The question of trust is back at the heart or our relationship: Can we trust each other again? The international context has changed. It's become worse on many levels, with tensions and dramatic crises. On top of it all, nine countries now have nuclear weapons, four of them situated in deeply unstable regions: North Korea, Pakistan, India, Israel.

Guillaume Serina's book seeks to build a bridge between yesterday and today. The detailed account of my meetings with President Ronald Reagan in Geneva and in Reykjavík, pieced together from interviews with some of the key participants and observers, puts in perspective what we tried to accomplish in Iceland: ridding the world of all nuclear weapons. Our meeting ended without an agreement on total elimination. But I am convinced, after the passage of three decades, that we did succeed in building a new model of negotiating the nature of our most deadly nuclear arsenals. The treaties and agreements that followed drastically reduced their numbers.

I suggested to President Reagan that he meet with us in Reykjavík in 1986 because I was very worried about the world's situation, and especially the state of relations between the two superpowers. A year earlier, we had met in Geneva. After difficult discussions, we adopted a joint statement which contained two central points. First, a nuclear war cannot be won and must never be fought. The second point, however, is equally important: the United States and the Soviet Union must not seek military superiority over the other.

My opinion from the beginning was that since the leaders of the two great powers agreed on these points, negotiations had to be conducted with the goal of moving immediately in this direction. We had to achieve, as soon as possible, radical cuts of nuclear weapons in all categories. But even after Geneva, the negotiations were not going well. Indeed, they were at a standstill.

Moreover, relations between our two countries were generally tense. They were routinely and dangerously being put to the test. In the spring of 1986, American warships entered our territorial waters in the Black Sea. We were forced to push them back. It was essential to break this negative cycle.

Our proposals were clear and concrete: cut in half the entire triad of strategic nuclear weapons; eliminate intermediate-range missiles in Europe; halt nuclear testing; agree on the demilitarization of space.

There were influential people in the Reagan administration who opposed the meeting. But the president accepted, making an important political choice. The discussions in Geneva between the two of us, which were attended by our foreign ministers, then broadened to include our experts, were concrete and productive.

We agreed on the main issues. Not only did we set a goal of a 50 percent cut in our nuclear arsenals in five years, but we agreed on the ultimate goal—a world without nuclear weapons. President Reagan said, "I am ready for that." I was also ready to sign such an agreement in principle right there in Reykjavík.

Sadly, this did not happen. The obstacle was the Strategic Defense Initiative (SDI), a project dear to Reagan. He insisted we give a green light to weapons tests in space. I could not agree. To agree on the elimination of weapons on Earth while at the same time opening an arms race in space was not acceptable to me.

That's how we parted. An agreement that could have been historic—a 50 percent reduction of the entire triad of nuclear weapons—had still not been signed. But at the press conference following our Reykjavík meeting, after thinking very seriously about the position we had reached during the negotiations, I told the hundreds of journalists who gathered there with high expectations: "It is not a failure, but a breakthrough. We looked beyond the horizon, to consider a world without nuclear weapons."

Subsequent events confirmed my judgment. The momentum of Reykjavík enabled us to sign, one year later, a treaty on the elimination of short and medium-range missiles. Let me insist on one key point that is generally underestimated: the ceilings and other elements agreed upon in Reykjavík began to take effect even before the formal treaties were signed. The total number of nuclear weapons stopped rising and major reductions were achieved in the three decades that have followed.

In 1991, President George H. W. Bush and I signed the first START (Strategic Arms Reduction Treaty). We also agreed to eliminate the majority of our tactical nuclear weapons. The implementation of the Reykjavík program was under way. It was a time of great accomplishments!

The most important element was that the agreements included an effective verification system. We said that we were prepared to accept stricter verification measures, but on a mutual basis. And these measures have brought stability and confidence for decades.

At the time we also set a pace of reduction that, if it had continued, could have led us far beyond where we are today toward a world free of nuclear weapons. Of course, we have had great successes. The Cold War was relegated to the past. The danger of a global nuclear conflict is no longer imminent. Thousands of nuclear weapons have been destroyed.

But a lot of very troubling elements remain. Nuclear arsenals are still very large and dangerous. Hundreds of nuclear weapons continue to be deployed in Europe. The treaty to end nuclear tests is not being enforced. New nations possessing the bomb have emerged, and there is a continuing threat of nuclear proliferation. New arms races have been launched before our eyes, and the threat of the militarization of space has returned to haunt us. The promise not to seek military superiority has been forgotten. One nation alone—the United States—accounts for almost half of the world's military spending.

If the situation continues, the goal of a world free of nuclear weapons will not be attainable. And one day, this weapon will explode.

What can we do to prevent this? We must demilitarize—demilitarize international relations, demilitarize political thinking. We need real progress that will prove to the world that the nuclear powers are complying with Article V of the Treaty on the Non-Proliferation of Nuclear Weapons: eliminating nuclear weapons. Nations' military budgets should be cut to a level only necessary to defend themselves. All countries should give up trying to gain military superiority. That's how I see things.

Some will say it's not realistic, it's utopian. But I must say that thirty years ago, many thought it was impossible to stop superpower confrontations, stop the arms race, and begin to eliminate entire stocks of weapons of war. Yet the leaders of two nuclear powers had the political will to act and the process began, despite all obstacles. What we need today is precisely this: political will. We need another level of leadership, collective leadership, of course. I want to be remembered as an optimist. Let us assimilate the lessons of the twentieth century in order to rid the world of this legacy in the twenty-first—the legacy of militarism, violence against peoples and nature, and weapons of mass destruction of all types.

This was the ultimate goal of Reykjavík which, as you will see in these pages, we came so very close to attaining.

# Prologue

◆

L ook out for the rattlesnakes." There are many warning signs. Fortunately, so far, only the six-foot tall Saguaro cactuses seem threatening. The midday sun is baking the dusty soil. At 109 degrees, it's not healthy to stay outside for very long. Only the distant mountains relieve the flat landscape that otherwise stretches to the horizon. The desert of southern Arizona, a few miles from the Mexican border, is most decidedly inhospitable. At ground level, all that's apparent in the foreground is an odd metallic structure with a large lid—a 700-ton armored hatch. And, 200 feet beyond, a lone staircase rushes into the entrails of what looks like the surface of the moon.

Suddenly, as we begin our descent of these stairs, it's cold. And dark. The metal staircase resounds under our footsteps.

The cage is gray. Warm lights, fixed to the wall, guide the way. At the bottom, fifty-eight steps, at least five stories down, there appears a succession of three armored doors, each secured with a magnetic locking system. But curiously, there is no real sense of claustrophobia. We are ninety feet beneath the desert, in the underground quarters of members of the US Air Force. At the end of the corridor sleeps a monster. A Titan II, to be precise, nestles in its silo—a nuclear missile, the biggest, most powerful, most destructive weapon ever created by man.

The beast is standing in a concrete cylinder eight feet thick and more than one hundred twenty feet deep. Its silo is maintained at a constant 60 degrees Fahrenheit, the optimal temperature for its particularly hazardous fuel mixture. The gray body looks like it has been plucked from another era: a smooth metal skin, bolts springing from its side, bristling with an array of pipes funneling in the fuel along its side, the huge vertical inscription "US Air Force." At the top of the rocket is a black cone, the nuclear warhead. Or rather the housing that once contained a warhead. This Titan II is disarmed.

The Titan II was in service from 1963 to 1986, deployed at three sites in Arkansas, Kansas, and Arizona. This particular example was installed in 1982 and is now classified as an "object"—the stilled heart of an underground base, which has become a museum. It is the only place in the United States that visitors today can penetrate to the heart of the American nuclear defense system of the Cold War era.

American nuclear missile bases are still organized, as they have been since they were first opened, into three large underground units: the rocket silo, the control room, and the living quarters (rudimentary bedrooms and a kitchen), all surrounding a staircase and elevator to the surface. These underground facilities are linked by a corridor lined with scores of pipes carrying air and water. The walls are painted the cold green of a surgeon's scrubs. The entire underground structure is built on enormous springs designed to attenuate the vibrations during the missile's launch—or accidental explosion.

In the control room, a central desk faces twelve metal computer racks. Everywhere, bright buttons are lit. The two service officers at the console have joint responsibility for the nuclear launch. The procedure is simple. The order is given by the commander in chief of the American armed forces, the president of the United States. The encrypted command is received at the base chosen to launch the nuclear missile. But the transmitted code is only part of the chain. It must be completed by instructions in a large red folder containing a six-digit code.

There remains one more decisive step before the launch. The two teammates at the missile base must each open a mini safe: one red, the other black. Each has only the combination of his or her own safe. Inside is a key. The senior of the two officers goes to one of the main computers and enters the six-digit code. At this point, the arm that holds the missile in the silo is lifted. The officer returns to the launch console and inserts his key. His assistant is on his left, six feet away, at an identical desk. Once the two keys are inserted, the countdown begins to resonate from the speakers. At zero, the two missileers turn their keys to the right.

The engines of the missile ignite. Their firepower is so intense that nine thousand gallons of water immediately rush into the tank to prevent the rocket from damaging itself. The propulsive force is equivalent to two Boeing 747s simultaneously taking off at full power. The Titan II begins to rise from its bed, the last remaining holding arms dropping away. Fifty-eight seconds after its code is entered, it is launched into the air. After five minutes of flight, at forty-five miles of altitude, it has exhausted its propellant. The missile then flies on, solely on launch momentum and its enormous kinetic energy.

Three targets are preprogrammed into its computers before launch. The actual destination code entered identifies only a single target. Even today, Cold War missile targets are classified top secret. But without too much difficulty, one can imagine that Moscow and perhaps a large Russian military base are still among those targets. Crossing the North Pole, it takes another twenty-five minutes for the Titan II to crash into Russia.

Missileers are the military personnel who have the ultimate responsibility for operating these infamous keys. They form a kind of fraternity within the US Air Force—men and women under enormous and unrelenting pressure. The potential destruction of an entire city and the death of thousands of people rests on them. What if they did not obey orders from above? In the 1983 film *Wargames*, the older of the duo, on receiving the order to launch, hesitates, then halts, a few seconds before the fateful zero of the countdown. His young assistant does not hesitate to kill him with a single bullet. It was only a training exercise.

What great pressure, being one of the two individuals to decide, at a single stroke, the elimination of hundreds of thousands of fellow members of the human race on the other side of the globe. Innocents. Victims of a purely political conflict, decided by two leaders hooked on their power. Could the *Wargames* scenario actually happen? Throughout the silo there are inscriptions on the walls proclaiming: "No lone zone. Two man policy mandatory." Impossible to be alone. In the event of an accident, the partner can help. Each shares domestic tasks, too. But they are colleagues, they are not really friends. Because they watch each other to prevent any stroke of madness or disobedience.

John Krumm was a missileer between 1980 and 1985, based at Grand Forks, North Dakota. "Most of us lived on the base, less than a mile from the elevator, where we used to go every morning," he says. "The first thing we did was to recite a series of different codes in phones to get into the silo. 'Good morning, Captain Krumm. I come to take over. X Ray Delta.' Then, a reply was heard. 'You are authenticated, you can enter.'"

For Captain Krumm and his fellow officers, under great pressure, often bone tired, thirty feet underground, theirs was a form of patriotic commitment. "My father fought in the North Atlantic during the Second World War," he says. "As for us, our mission was: 'Mutually Assured Destruction'—guarantors of the US nuclear deterrent. I saw officers crack because of the pressure of this profession."

His colleague John Gazelius continues, "People [missileers] are not greeted with enthusiasm when they return home. It's a very methodical job, where we have to sit and wait until something terrible happens. Nothing, apparently, very spectacular. Just the interminable wait, in a bunker underground, a few feet from a nuclear bomb. Not the work of Mr. Everyone, that's for sure."

The training of these officers is not taken lightly. Everything is done to test their will to assimilate their duties and perform their tasks that are so particular. They are shown a deeply disturbing film about the aftermath of the bombings of Hiroshima and Nagasaki. The interview also includes an extensive psychological test. John Krumm still remembers the examiner's questions:

"Have you ever thought about suicide and how would you get rid of yourself?" his interrogator asks.

"I never thought of suicide. I do not have an answer to your question."

"Do not hide anything. You've thought about it, because everybody thinks about it at some point."

"I must be abnormal, I never thought of it."

"I cannot validate your test if you do not answer me."

"I can't help you."

"You've just passed your psychological assessment."

These missileers are the last links in the chain of command that starts with the president of the United States. Each must have a blank state of mind. "During all the time I served, I would have launched the missile. There is no doubt that I would have started a nuclear war," Krumm says today. "I think I was lying to my consciousness, convincing myself that I was doing something moral. But in a way, I made a pact with the devil."

American missiles are still in operation. The nuclear weapon did not disappear with the end of the Soviet Union. But today, US nuclear deterrence is based on three launch platforms: undetectable submarines; mobile and furtive bombers; and underground bases, not unlike the one that is now a museum in Arizona. This last leg of what is known as the "triad" is highly criticized as a source of enormous risk for neighboring populations in the event of an accident or terrorist attack. Their main weakness: All supposed enemies of the United States know their location.

But in the 1980s, in the middle of the Cold War, Ronald Reagan's America counted on these silos. The Kremlin of Brezhnev, then Andropov, Chernenko, and finally Gorbachev had mastery over the massive conventional forces of the Red Army. Then, intermediate-range missiles SS-18 and SS-20 were installed in the Asian part of the USSR and just behind the Iron

Curtain in Eastern Europe. In 1982, with the support of their NATO allies, the Americans countered by placing Pershing II missiles in West Germany. Today, the tension between the United States and Russia is such that nuclear missiles are on the verge of a launch into orbit.

The following chapters describe in previously undisclosed detail an episode little-known to the general public. An odd, frigid weekend in Iceland, in the middle of October more than thirty years ago. And a barely believable poker game between the leaders of the world's two biggest nuclear powers on this icy, neutral terrain. The challenge: the total elimination of nuclear weapons. The characters: Ronald Reagan and Mikhail Gorbachev. Two strong leaders, who played with the destiny of the world in a tiny house barely 160 miles from the Arctic Circle.

# ONE

# *In the Reagan White House*

One degree above zero, Fahrenheit: not the polar-like temperature of Moscow on January 21, 1985, but rather Washington, DC, on the northern fringe of the American south, a few steps from the Atlantic Ocean. In the summer, the American capital is hot and humid. But in winter, it is equally pitiless. By noontime, the wind has subsided after a midwinter blizzard.

The old man who steps forward is dressed in a dark blue suit, a white shirt and a navy-blue tie, with red and white stripes. Ronald Wilson Reagan, who will celebrate his seventy-fourth birthday in two weeks, becomes the oldest president of the

United States as he takes the oath of office to begin his second term. And on this day he looks every inch his age. At his side, his second wife, Nancy, is wearing an electric blue suit.

Reelected in November 1984, he triumphed over his Democratic opponent, Walter Mondale, in what can only be called a landslide—carrying forty-nine of the fifty states. Minnesota, Mondale's home, was the only state to escape the Reagan juggernaut. Of 54.4 million votes cast, just 37.5 million were for Mondale, a loss of 58.8 percent to 40.6 percent. A humiliation.

The results of his first term of office had convinced Americans that Ronald Reagan should be awarded a second term. He'd managed to bring inflation back to an acceptable single-digit level, compared with 13 percent when he took office. Unemployment had also fallen between 1981 and 1985. But the price of this success was an enormous tax cut which benefited the richest and caused the national debt to balloon to $1 trillion, with accumulating annual deficits reaching $100 billion.

Reagan had officially taken the oath the day before, on January 20, as mandated by the Constitution. The brief, televised ceremony took place in the grand foyer of the White House. This day falling on a Sunday, the public inauguration ceremony was scheduled for Monday. At least a 140 thousand tickets have been distributed for the event. Ronald Reagan enjoys an incredible reserve of support from the American people. Many moderate Democrats voted for the Republican president. But the organizers preferred, just twelve hours before the investiture, to cancel the outdoor festivities, though thousands have assembled anyway on the National Mall, braving the bone-chilling cold. Instead, it has been moved to the Capitol, under the cupola, where the fresco of the Italian artist Constantino Brumidi, *The Apotheosis of Washington*, watches over him, that Reagan takes his place before Warren E. Burger, chief justice of the Supreme Court. Reagan lays his left hand on the Bible, raises his right hand, and declares: "I, Ronald Wilson Reagan, solemnly swear that I will faithfully carry out the office of president of the United States and that to the best of my ability I shall preserve, protect and defend the Constitution of the United States." The president then turns to deliver his second inaugural address.

Commentators expect few real surprises. A president has officially arrived yet again in office, but this is a second term. The same team around Reagan, more or less, will be reappointed. No change, either, from a political perspective. Have not the American people re-elected a team? As the saying goes, "you don't change a winning team."

## Well-filled Days

Reagan, ignoring his age, plays the role and the reality of the presidency to the hilt. His typical working day begins relatively early, with breakfast taken at 7:45 with his wife Nancy, in his private apartments in the White House. The president usually chooses cereals, fresh fruit, and decaffeinated coffee. Then, direct to the Oval Office, decorated in a sober style. A wide cream-colored carpet warms the room, setting off the great seal of the president embroidered into the center. First item: the president's daily briefing on the security of the United States. In general, he is joined by the White House chief of staff and the national security adviser, the briefing on the state of the world, crises, and key issues by the director of the Central Intelligence Agency (CIA) or one of his top aides, often joined by the secretary of defense and the secretary of state. Then, as now, the content is based on cables from American diplomats, reports from CIA agents and analysts, and foreign-based military personnel. For about twenty minutes, or more if necessary, Reagan receives a global synthesis from the world's most elaborate intelligence system.

The president's day then continues with in-house meetings and public events, speeches, travel around Washington, and planning for future trips across the nation and the world. When the president receives a foreign head of state, this daily routine is preempted by an official meeting with photographs in the Oval Office, usually followed by a joint press conference. If it is a state visit, the ultimate bilateral showcase, an elaborate banquet is set up in the gardens, or the East Room—the largest room of the White House—with a candlelit dinner where tuxedos and evening dresses are mandatory.

On a routine day, though, the president's activities are planned minutely, tightly scheduled, minute-by-minute. Take for example, Tuesday, October 7, 1986. An internal White House document details the process: "Breakfast with selected Congressmen; appointment with J. Miller; signing ceremony for S. J. Res. 159; NSPG meeting; photo with candidates for governor; meeting with Yuri Orlov; briefing with human rights leaders; appointment with Senator Chic Hecht; dinner for the Republican Governors Association."

While on the road, the president's schedule is modified, but is not necessarily lighter. On Monday, September 29, 1986, for example, he travels to two Midwestern cities—Kansas City, Missouri, and Sioux Falls, South Dakota. But on that day, he also needs to devote time to the following subjects: tax reform; a meeting with Secretary of State George Shultz and president of Georgia Eduard Shevardnadze; and sanctions against South Africa's apartheid regime.

To unwind, Ronald Reagan likes to play with Rex, his King Charles spaniel.

## A Heterogeneous Team

At the beginning of his second term, Ronald Reagan has surrounded himself with is a small cadre of veterans of American politics and the Republican Party. His closest advisor is Donald Regan. A virtual namesake, absent two letters, blessed with a perfect understanding of the president's psychology. Having advised Reagan since his days as governor of California from 1967 to 1975, Regan was appointed White House chief of staff in 1985. "I will now be in charge of the whole ball of wax," he remarks. This former businessman has Reagan's ear and confidence. Legend has it that he arrives every morning in the Oval Office with a fresh joke, to start the day in a good mood.

Regardless, he always confides that his principal role is to prepare the president for his meetings, just as a movie star is prepared for a day's filming. It's necessary that "the star has everything he needs to shine." He sees his scheduling as a type of script in which the characters come and go, where the scenes are repeated and played, and where the plot unfolds one day after another.

Donald Regan, a key figure in the administration until his resignation in 1987, is a pure product of the American dream. Born in Cambridge, Massachusetts, he was the son of an Irish police officer. His fate changed when he received a scholarship to study at Harvard University. He majored in English, then entered Harvard Law School, but he never graduated. Instead he dropped out to join the Marines, rising to lieutenant colonel and serving in the Pacific during World War II. After the war, he joined Merrill Lynch in 1946, as a junior account executive, climbing the ranks until 1971, when he became chairman and CEO, before joining Governor Reagan in Sacramento. When Reagan was elected president, Regan was appointed secretary of the treasury, placed in charge of carrying out "Reaganism," the economic policy that slashed taxes for the rich, hoping to create a surge in new jobs.

From his first arrival in Washington, Donald Regan faced a host of opponents. Coming from Wall Street, he was met with considerable skepticism by most of the professional political class and permanent bureaucracy that comprised the Washington elite. More surprising, and significant, when he arrived in the White House as chief of staff, he found himself rubbing first lady Nancy Reagan the wrong way as she sought to influence her husband's schedule, traditionally controlled by the chief of staff. Under the influence of a San Francisco astrologer, Nancy Reagan sought to save the president from crucial appointments during days with bad omens. This unnerved Regan immensely.

National security advisor Robert McFarlane did not come from the same mold. He was a soldier, born in Texas. He entered the US Naval Academy in Annapolis at the age of eighteen—for him, the military was a vocation and a calling. After graduation, he joined the Marine Corps, serving two tours in Vietnam and was decorated with the Bronze Star. At the end of the war, he joined the White House Fellows program, becoming a young military adviser to Henry Kissinger, then national security advisor to President Nixon.

By 1980, McFarlane had joined Reagan's campaign for president, largely responsible for his foreign policy platform. During his first term in office, Reagan named McFarlane counselor to

Secretary of State Alexander Haig, then special envoy to the Middle East, responsible for Israeli-Palestinian issues, against the background of the civil war in Lebanon, where he successfully pressed for the United States to become involved. Three years later, McFarlane was appointed national security advisor.

At the Pentagon, Caspar Weinberger is Ronald Reagan's secretary of defense. Born in San Francisco, a Republican to the core, Weinberger served during the Second World War on the Pacific front.

At the start of Reagan's first term, American diplomacy was headed by Secretary of State Alexander Haig. With the background and discipline of an army general, Haig also knew intimately the inner workings of the White House, having served as chief of staff for presidents Richard Nixon and Gerald Ford, before being sent to NATO as supreme commander of Allied Forces in Europe. Throughout, Haig was deeply involved with developing America's relations with its most important allies, particularly the United Kingdom, France, and West Germany. But Haig clashed frequently with several of Reagan's leading advisors, particularly Weinberger and McFarlane. By the summer of 1982, he was gone.

A replacement was needed immediately. Reagan turned to a one-time secretary of the treasury who had served under President Richard Nixon. An economist, George Pratt Shultz was scarcely familiar with America's global network of diplomats. His career had begun as a professor at the Massachusetts

Institute of Technology (MIT) and at the University of Chicago before Nixon brought him to Washington. When Reagan turned to him as his chief diplomat, Shultz was immediately plunged into the chaos of Lebanon, the toxic nuances of the Cold War, and a host of instabilities in Latin America.

## Ronald Reagan, a Star of Politics

This palace guard of a cabinet does its best to influence the decisions of the president on a daily basis. Reagan has common sense, but he does not necessarily have the details of every issue at his fingertips. During his eight years in office, he manages his team deftly, but gently. Reagan does not appreciate conflicts between people and tries to avoid them at all costs—sometimes to his own detriment.

Born into a modest family in Illinois on February 6, 1911, Ronald Reagan is one of those historical figures who seized opportunities throughout his life. "Forcing fate," could be his motto. On his desk at the White House is a wooden plaque engraved with an inscription. It faces his guests with a silent pledge: "It can be done."

In rural Tampico, Illinois, the son of Nelle and John Reagan had a childhood without apparent difficulty. He liked to swim in the nearby river with his brother Neil, who was two years older. The Reagan family moved often. John was a sales representative for a shoe manufacturer and Nelle cared for the children, while doing the sewing. At the time, housing in rural areas had no running water or toilets, so the family lived in conditions similar to the modest origins of its ancestors. On the paternal side, the Reagans fled the potato famine in Ireland in the nineteenth century. The maternal branch, the Wilsons, were a mixture of Scottish and English. Nelle was the youngest daughter of seven children. The value of work well-done and the Christian faith were a deep, daily center of their lives.

Ronald applied himself as a student. At age eleven, he saw his first play and was thrilled, promptly discovering a taste and talent for the theater. At Dixon High School, a hundred miles west of Chicago, he earned high marks. In high school, he was president of the theater club and captain of the football team. An athletic teen, he loved sports, and he also joined the rescue brigade on the Rock River, a tributary of the Mississippi. At eighteen, Ronald Wilson Reagan left the family nest to enroll in Eureka College in Eureka, Illinois. At the time, only 7 percent of young Americans pursued higher education. His majors were sociology and economics, but he spent most of his time at the theater, on the football field, in the swimming pool, and on the running track.

So it was hardly surprising that his first job as a radio commentator for baseball and football combined his skills and interests. It was 1932 and the United States was in in the depths of the Great Depression. After failing to find work at a radio station in Chicago, he got his first job in nearby Davenport, Iowa. He moved up quickly to the state capital, Des Moines. At the age of twenty-three, Reagan began to make a name for himself in the Midwest through radio.

During a trip to California with the Chicago Cubs baseball team, Reagan decided to stay in Los Angeles. He had already accompanied the team twice in Catalina Island in California during their winter retreat. In 1937, he took advantage of his third stay to visit the prestigious Biltmore Hotel in downtown Los Angeles. His friend Joy Rodgers, who had worked beside him for the radio station WHO and was now a singer, introduced him to a Hollywood agent. On Joy's advice, Ronald did not wear his glasses, so he couldn't see very much. But his stature and his élan were enough to convince the agent to take Reagan on. Reagan's agent landed him a screen test for him at Warner Brothers, which was followed by a seven-year contract at $200 a week—a respectable $3,500 in today's currency.

## An Honest Hollywood Career

Reagan's Hollywood career lasted two decades. When it was interrupted by World War II, he shot training films for the Air Force. Apart from that, he bounced between westerns, war movies, and romantic comedies. It was a steady and honest career, largely in B movies. Between 1937 and 1964, Reagan appeared in sixty-nine films and twenty-two television soap operas—great experience in front of the camera, which would serve him well during his political career. Still, Reagan never landed a single starring role that could have made him a true celebrity of the screen.

Alongside his acting career, Reagan became involved with politics. Post-war America had become virulently anti-Communist, though the enclave of Hollywood had a reputation for being socially liberal and politically left wing. Between 1953 and 1962, Reagan became the official presenter of a television series sponsored by General Electric. At the beginning of each of the over two hundred episodes, which consisted of twenty-tree minute vignettes, Reagan appeared on the small screen to introduce the program that would follow, along with advertisements for his employer.

Although Reagan was a "representative" of a major brand, he was also twice elected president of Hollywood's powerful actors' union, the Screen Actors Guild (SAG), serving from 1947 to 1952 and again from 1959 to 1960. But it was earlier, in the 1940s that Reagan took a fateful first step, becoming an informer for the Federal Bureau of Investigation (FBI), along with his first wife, the actress Jane Wyman. Under the code name of T-10, he denounced a host of actors he believed to be Communists. In October 1947, he testified before the House Un-American Activities Committee.

## Governor of California

By 1964, Reagan's acting career was coming to an end, and he embarked on a political career. He was already involved in

Republican activism. Unsurprisingly, he began at the top with a campaign for governor of California. Victory in the Republican primary led to the general election on November 8, 1966, against the outgoing governor, Democrat Pat Brown, father of future governor Jerry Brown. The result was a million-vote tidal wave victory, thanks to the exceptional mobilization of Californian conservative voters. During his first term, Governor Reagan took a hard line against the antiwar demonstrations against the Vietnam War that were sweeping state campuses. He also assembled opposition within the Republican Party to Richard Nixon, former vice president of Dwight Eisenhower, in his campaign for president. But without success. Nixon was elected to his first term as president in 1968.

Reagan easily won reelection to four more years as governor on November 3, 1970. But quietly, behind the scenes, he began preparing a campaign of quite another magnitude.

## Candidate for the White House . . . First Time

Most Americans started to discover Ronald Reagan when he began unveiling his campaign for the presidency in 1975 and 1976. At this moment in American political history, the presidency was particularly weak. The Watergate scandal had seen to that. Richard Nixon resigned in August 1974, and the United States moved from the "imperial presidency" to a more powerful Congress and a hesitant executive. Gerald Ford, Nixon's vice president, came to power after his predecessor's resignation. The former Michigan congressman embodied a moderate Republicanism, which found little real place in post-Vietnam America. But the Democratic Party was also divided and did not seem to offer any serious alternative.

The principal opposition to Gerald Ford in his campaign for reelection in his own right came from within the Republican Party, in the person of Ronald Reagan. The former governor of California succeeded in a parade of Republican primary contests, and the Republican National Convention, held in Kansas City from August 16 to 19, was an "open convention," with delegates, all uncommitted, free to decide between the two men. In the sports arena that housed this steaming convention, Ford snatched the nomination with a margin of just 117 votes out of more than 2,100 delegates.

But on this evening of August 19, the star turned out to be the loser. At the insistence of the crowd, President Ford signaled to Reagan, watching from the stands, to come down on stage to speak. The former actor rose, but signaled the cheering delegates to sit down. Still, they continued to shout, "Speech, speech!" Reagan, who'd just lost the nomination, arrived on stage, accompanied by his second wife, Nancy, "without having any idea what he was going to say," she would later confide.

What followed marked the actual launch of his national political career. Improvising a speech broadcast live on national television in prime time, Reagan laid the groundwork for his success four years later. "I had an assignment the other day," he began. "Someone asked me to write a letter for a time capsule that is going to be opened in Los Angeles a hundred years from now, on our Tricentennial . . . We live in a world in which the great powers have poised and aimed at each other horrible missiles of destruction, nuclear weapons that can in a matter of minutes arrive at each other's country and destroy, virtually, the civilized world we live in. And suddenly it dawned on me, those who would read this letter a hundred years from now will know whether those missiles were fired. They will know whether we met our challenge. Whether they have the freedoms that we have known up until now will depend on what we do here."

This dream of eliminating nuclear weapons, pronounced candidly and improvised that night, would become Ronald Reagan's highest priority during his presidency.

In November 1976, Gerald Ford was defeated by Democrat Jimmy Carter.

## What Vision of the World?

"America is back." Reagan's slogan for his 1980 campaign meant at once everything and nothing. But it must be understood in the context of his opponent, the Democratic incumbent, Jimmy Carter. Perceived as a nonleader, an executive holding an office substantially weakened in the wake of the Watergate scandal that drove Nixon from power, Carter had established a new vision of international relations revolving around human rights. In this context, he brought Israel and Egypt together in the Camp David Accords. But the seizure of American hostages by students backing the newly installed ruling mullahs in Tehran, Iran, demonstrated the limits of a pedagogical, but not very charismatic or authoritative, president.

Ronald Reagan was elected easily, bringing to the office his attitude of champion. He flexed his anti-Communist muscles, establishing a leadership role for the United States in what had become a "frozen" cold war; his opponent, an aging, ill, and deeply conservative Leonid Brezhnev, was helpless at the end of his reign. Still, American foreign policy revolved around the Soviet Union. And the new president, from the moment he was installed in power, began seeking his own path. "Reagan was convinced that U.S. presidents refrained from openly criticizing the Soviet Union hoping to cooperate with it," wrote Jack Matlock, one of his advisors on the National Security Council. "Would it not have been better," Reagan wondered, "if Franklin Roosevelt had been more candid about the nature of the alliance with the Soviet Union?" And Reagan was prepared to criticize Stalinism more harshly.

## A Charming President, but After?

Was Reagan the public man different from Reagan the private man? Nearly fifteen years after his death, a certain enigma remains around the president. Did the former actor have the intellectual level that the office requires? How did he make up for his lack of education or training for this position as a world leader? Was he a hard worker, or the dilettante joker as he has sometimes been described? It seems he was all of this at once.

"As president, Reagan was almost always as pleasant as possible," wrote Sarah McClendon, long-serving White House correspondent and who covered eleven presidents. "Everyone loved him. You could not do otherwise. I knew a lot of congressmen who would come to the White House. 'I will tell him what I think,' and then finally said nothing. They sat, listened to his jokes and allowed themselves to be neutralized. Many journalists were taken in, in the same way."

John Poindexter, the national security advisor from 1985, delivers an enlightening view of Reagan, the man: "There is one aspect that people do not realize about Reagan. They see him as an extrovert. But in reality, he was introverted. Inside the Oval Office, with only two or three people around him, the president was very calm, thoughtful, self-assured. But when he got out of the office, it was as if he were coming on stage. He became an extrovert. He was not pretending. He just put on his little makeup. This is what made him a great communicator." Poindexter also remembers the presidential weekends spent at Reagan's California ranch near Santa Barbara. "The White House team stayed in town and only went to the ranch in an emergency. He remained there to cut wood with his old friends, to ride a horse. An introverted nature. That was the real man behind the scenes. And I am convinced that his having been an actor was a very good preparation to be president."

# TWO

## *Gorba . . . Who?*

I ts rectangular paving stones have felt soldiers' boots, tanks' treads, wheels of countless Red Army military vehicles, and the millions of tourists who, since the fall of the Communist regime, have also paraded across them in ever growing numbers. But Red Square, in the historical heart of Moscow, retains its mysteries—unchanged for a thousand years. The Cathedral of St. Basil and its colorful bell towers are visible from afar on the horizon, while the Kremlin shelters behind its high red walls, topped by medieval battlements. The golden dome is visible above a yellow building housing the Duma, the nation's parliament and the offices where the president of the Russian Federation rules.

Planted directly beneath the walls, looming onto the square, the dark marble mausoleum of Vladimir Ilyich Lenin continues to bear witness to the country's Communist past. From there, the embalmed body of the father of the Bolshevik Revolution of 1917, the founder of the Soviet regime, watches over a nation as a historical relic. But Lenin and his successors still seem to be everywhere. His mausoleum served as a balcony for Soviet dignitaries to admire their military parades. On its walls Stalin, Khrushchev, Brezhnev, and their entourages showed themselves to the world's cameras, then turned to watch, tall and proud, as the might of their armed forces rolled past them.

Even today, the high walls of the Kremlin are home to many secrets, this fortress at once fascinating and intriguing. The Kremlin estate contains sixty-nine acres of palaces, gardens, and churches. Its first buildings date to the eleventh century, on a hill where Russian archaeologists have found signs of houses still standing. But it was at the turn of the century in the year 1500 that the Kremlin began to take on its present form with the construction, one after the other, of a collection of grand palaces. Ivan III, also known as Ivan the Great, became the Grand Prince of all the Russias—the first to unify this immense, heterogeneous territory. The Kremlin eventually became the residence of the tsars, then the Soviet leaders after the Revolution of 1917. Today the complex comprises more than twenty buildings—palaces, cathedrals, and churches—each tower bearing a name. In 1561, Ivan the Terrible (the fourth Ivan) had St. Basil's built next door—then, legend has it, ordered the eyes of its architect put out so that it could never be matched, earning himself a name that would echo through the centuries and set a marker for future rulers of Russia.

Stalin preferred the long building of the Grand Palace of the Kremlin on the side facing the Moskva River. Some believe he changed rooms every night, acutely paranoid that he would be assassinated as he slept. Inside the Kremlin, this building abuts Cathedral Place, where four exquisite Orthodox Christian structures rival each other for their architectural and artistic beauty. The tsars were crowned in the Cathedral of the Assumption, the oldest and the first to be built, in 1470, from native stone. On the other side of the central esplanade of the Kremlin, the triangular Senate building houses the presidential apartments, and stands next to the Supreme Soviet. Diagonally opposite, the modern building of the State Palace houses the meeting hall where the congresses of the ruling Communist Party of the Soviet Union (CPSU) took place.

From this hill overlooking the city, inside the red ramparts, the feeling of power is ever present. The Russian capital exudes the power that has marked every turn of its history. The Empire of the Tsars. Then the Soviet Empire. The majesty of Red Square, the heaviness of the Duma (its parliament), and the elegance of the Bolshoi Theater. Everything is here. Isolated from so much of the vast territory it commands, especially during the long Russian winters. Moscow is 400 miles from St. Petersburg, the nation's second largest city, and more than a thousand miles from other major European capitals.

Flashback. The bell rings. Ten o'clock in the morning. The dial of the clock of the Tower of the Savior, whose red star shines at its summit tells the hour. The crowd is standing at attention. On the mausoleum of Lenin, the members of the Central Committee of the Communist Party have arrived. Everyone stares at one man. He wears a dark gray raincoat, though there's no rain, a hat and eyeglasses of the same color. Mikhail Gorbachev smiles slightly and greets the audience with a gesture of the right hand. In front of him, an immense, three-story tall portrait of Lenin on a red background is suspended on the facade of the department store Gum across the square. Below, men in uniforms and ordinary citizens.

"Parade! Your attention! Prepare for the procession. Eyes left!" A voice thunders from the loudspeakers. At this moment, an immense Soviet-made convertible enters Red Square. Marshal Sergey Leonidovich Sokolov stands, saluting. He is the minister of defense of the Soviet Union and reviews the troops of the Red Army.

On May 9, 1985, Soviet leaders celebrate the fortieth anniversary of the end of the "Great Patriotic War," as they call World War II. Without the Soviet victory against the Nazis on the Eastern front, the history of the twentieth century would have been quite different. But while the tanks and the missile-carrying trucks roll through this square of more than seventeen acres, Russian and foreign viewers have eyes only for Gorbachev. He arrived as the Soviet leader in March, just two months earlier. And the West is discovering a man far younger than his predecessors.

When Ronald Reagan began his second term in January 1985, the master of the Kremlin was still Konstantin Chernenko. Aged seventy-four, he was a glaring example of the gerontocracy that had paralyzed the Soviet system. The USSR had previously been led by Leonid Brezhnev, who had taken office in October 1964, and whose reign lasted until November 1982. The Communist Party's general secretary was nearly seventy-six years old at his death, but it was apparent that his diminishing faculties had long since eroded his once iron will. A fossilization of power had come to grip Moscow, rendering the Kremlin incapable of engaging in the least reform, cut off from a society that was straining to evolve.

Yuri Andropov, the first head of the KGB to rule the country, succeeded Brezhnev. Already almost seventy when he took over, he would remain in power only fifteen months before succumbing to kidney problems. Finally, it was Chernenko's turn to be "elected" head of the Party, and therefore ruler of the nation. "After Andropov's death, there was a disappointment that Gorbachev was not named to the top post instead of Chernenko,' says Roald Sagdeev, a nuclear physicist and subsequent Gorbachev advisor. There began an era of stagnation. Chernenko had been best known for overseeing the construction a few years earlier of the nuclear bunker, the bomb shelter beneath the Kremlin. "In the early 1980s, the Americans had deployed Pershing missiles in Europe and this had scared Moscow," Sagdeev recalls, "because these nuclear missiles could reach our capital in just a few minutes, not in twenty-five or thirty minutes, as would have been the case with intercontinental missiles fired from North America. In short, the construction of the bunker became an urgent priority."

"The successive disappearances of Brezhnev and Andropov have somewhat clarified the rules governing the choice of secretaries-general of the Party," French Sovietologist Patrice Gélard explained at the time. The general secretary is always a member of the Political Bureau (Politburo), secretary of the party Central Committee, and chairman of the commission in charge of organizing the funeral of the deceased general secretary. He was not necessarily the immediate deputy of his predecessor (as was Andropov) but was most often (Khrushchev and Chernenko) the first among equals. Nevertheless, the choice of Chernenko by his peers in the Political Bureau suggested, as is the case with every change, that the general secretary ensured the representation of the different interest groups in the Party (party apparatus, administration, army, police and KGB, as well as the main Soviet republics). If Stalin and Khrushchev appeared to be true leaders of the Soviet Union, Brezhnev, despite all the manifold honors bestowed on him, never succeeded in giving this impression. Andropov did not have sufficient time to cement himself in power.

Chernenko, who had smoked since the age of nine, died after only thirteen months at the head of the Soviet empire. For many dignitaries, it was time to move on to a new generation—to rejuvenate and reform. The time of a certain Mikhail Gorbachev had arrived. "Before he was general secretary and since Andropov, there had already been many stories about him," recalls Roald Sagdeev, who subsequently worked closely with Gorbachev. The stories spread not in the still tightly state-controlled press, but among the intellectual elite of Moscow. Andropov had asked Gorbachev to supervise a working group on the future of the country. Gorbachev divided this group in half: one group on the defense and military (arms race, nuclear issues) and another more economical, examining how to overcome the stagnation that had descended on the nation under Brezhnev and never lifted. From that moment, Gorbachev became very popular in the heart of the Politburo.

Since the dictatorship of Stalin (1924–1953), the "political bureau" was the most powerful organ among all Soviet institutions. It would also play a key role in Gorbachev's foreign policy. At the Eighteenth Congress of the CPSU in 1939, "Stalin announced that new [purges] were no longer necessary and denounced [excesses] committed in recent years," says Nicolas Werth, a French historian specializing in the Soviet Union.

"The centralization of the Party was strengthened, with the Politburo reinforcing its preeminence over all other governing bodies." But during the Stalin's rule "between March 1939 and October 1952," Werth continues, "the Party's governing bodies are systematically ignored: no congress is held for thirteen and a half years, no plenum of the Central Committee for five and a half years. The Politburo (ten full members and four alternates) itself seldom gathers. In the present state of our still fragmentary knowledge of decision-making at the highest level, it is difficult to say to what extent Stalin was really the autocrat deciding everything, as Nikita Khrushchev [his successor] later suggested, or a skilled arbiter among different rival groups."

Later, under the leadership of Leonid Brezhnev (1964–1982), two forces rose to power: the army, which impacts both "the great political and economic choices as well as the often-contrasting options of the foreign policy of the USSR in the years 1965–1985," Werth suggests. In 1976, "Brezhnev took the title of Marshal of the USSR. Donning this uniform, the Party's leading dignitary solemnly affirmed the convergence of the interests of the Party and the army. At the same time, it appropriated, for the benefit of the Party, the military's prestige, which occupied a very high place in the regime's values."

In 1977, the Soviet Union adopted a new constitution to consolidate the power of an aging, worn-out team. In 1980, the average age of Politburo members was seventy-one years old. The new constitution's text "insisted more clearly than the previous constitutions on the leading role of the Communist Party," Werth observes. The document further legalized the Party as "the leading force and guide of Soviet society, the nucleus of its political system, the state and all social organizations."

## A "Youth" Comes to Power

So, when Gorbachev assumed power on March 11, 1985, Westerners were surprised by the "youth" of the new Soviet leader, who had just celebrated his fifty-fourth birthday. Immediately, the news was perceived as a sign of a new era, with the Soviet leader as a potential partner. Or at least as someone to talk to. Most of the world's leaders meet him for the first time on the day of Chernenko's Kremlin funeral on March 13, 1985. "The atmosphere and tone were direct, precise, interesting," French president François Mitterrand confided to journalists. "He is a solid, calm, fair-minded man who already has a firm grasp of his office, approaching his duties with a will to take hold of events, so that he's able to treat the world's most difficult situations with audacity and precision."

"Everyone," said Hubert Védrine, diplomatic adviser to the French president, "noticed that he did not say a word to Gromyko, who stood motionless, with a tense smile, understanding who was in charge."

The Americans, too, were favorably impressed by Gorbachev's sudden rise to power, anticipating that "we finally have someone to work with," as one Reagan advisor put it. The first meeting of Russian and American leaders also dates from the funeral of Chernenko, where Vice President George H. W. Bush represented the United States. An appointment was scheduled that same evening with Gorbachev and his top aides. "Gorbachev began with a gracious word, thanking us for paying tribute to Secretary General Chernenko," recalls Secretary of State George Shultz. "Then he launched into a declaration that went the furthest on foreign policy than I have heard so far, on the part of a Soviet leader."

The new Russian leader warned his American guests: "The United States must understand that there will be continuity both from an internal and an external point of view in the Soviet Union." He then glanced at several cards prepared for him, but quickly tossed them aside, according to Shultz, looking Bush in the eye, and declaring: "The USSR never intended to fight the United States and still does not have this intention today. There have never been fools in the Soviet leadership and there are still none."

In a top-secret memorandum for Reagan from McFarlane, the national security advisor described Gorbachev's character, style, and ulterior motives as "like no other previous leader of the Soviet Union before." Gorbachev, McFarlane continued, seemed to have a "more pragmatic" and dynamic approach. "He has more confidence in himself, even arrogance . . . about his ability to revitalize the Soviet system, reach agreements with foreign leaders and regain credibility with diplomacy."

In the same document, McFarlane examined the public image of Gorbachev, after barely eight months in power. "According to a source with contacts in the Leningrad media, Gorbachev viewed all the images shot during his visit to select what was to be broadcast. [Indian] Prime Minister Gandhi was also struck during his visit to Moscow by the way Gorbachev played photographers."

Beyond the image gradually emerging of the new Soviet leader, the Americans were trying to understand the new political inflection Gorbachev was planning for the Soviet Union. "He warned that accelerated economic growth and industrial modernization are imperative if the USSR wants to compete in the global market," Reagan wrote.

## An All-Soviet Route

If Gorbachev was younger, dynamic, and, in a word, different from his predecessors, he was nevertheless a pure product of the Soviet system—born to a family of farmers from the North Caucasus, with mixed Russian and Ukrainian origins, and a tragic past. His grandparents, accused of being Trotskyites, lived through famine and purges. Gorbachev was born in Privolnoye, in the territory of Stavropol. His father was a worker on a collective farm and, when the Germans occupied the region in 1942, he enlisted in the Red Army. Meanwhile, young Mikhail began working on the farm. At the end of the war he was hired as a combine harvester. But this life did not suit him. He worked hard at school, excelled, and applied to the nation's leading institution, Moscow State University. He was accepted immediately, a tribute to his career as a young farm worker and a national medal for being one of the youngest farmers in the country. He then automatically joined the Communist Party. "My years at university were not only extremely interesting, but also a period of intensive work. I had to catch up with a lot of things. I knew I had gaps in my education, coming from a rural school," he would recall later. "But frankly, I always had a lot of ambition."

The university was a pivotal period in the development of the future general secretary and president of the USSR. "The University of Moscow gave me the fundamental knowledge and intellectual training that determined my career. This is where the reevaluation of the history of my country, its present and its future began," he said. It was also at this time that he met Raisa Titarenko, whom he married three years later, in 1953.

Gorbachev graduated with a law degree two years afterwards. He then returned to Stavropol to begin his career as a lawyer: first at the office of the local prosecutor, then at the offices of the Communist Party, which ran all operations in the region. From the 1970s, Gorbachev began to establish his influence—developing economic programs to stimulate agricultural production, overseeing construction of an airport accommodating large planes that allowed a direct connection with Moscow. Stavropol is more than seven hundred miles from the capital, and the harsh climate, especially in winter, complicates land transport.

November 27, 1978, marked a turning point in his career. The Central Committee of the CPSU appointed him as its secretary. The Gorbachev family, Raisa and now a daughter, Irina, moved to Moscow. From then on, Gorbachev's ascent was dazzling. He quickly became a member of the Central Committee, then the ruling Politburo. But the context was most complex, even toxic. The health of Leonid Brezhnev was declining, and behind the scenes the titanic struggles to decide his successor intensified. Andrei Gromyko, Viktor Grishin, Yuri Andropov, and Konstantin Chernenko were all involved. Gorbachev seemed appreciated by all, but was too young.

"On the political level, Brezhnevism was nothing more than a conservative reaction to Khrushchev's attempt to reform the authoritarian model prevailing in the country," Gorbachev wrote in his memoirs. Brezhnev knew the state of mind of the party elites intimately, as well as the state of the military-industrial complex. He provided unlimited support for a policy designed simply to revive the system inherited from Stalin. The two short mandates of Andropov and Chernenko followed. In March 1985, the time for Mikhail Gorbachev struck.

"When I became general secretary on March 11, 1985, I was immediately confronted with an avalanche of problems," he noted later. "We had to improve our relations with the West, particularly with the United States, and put an end to the arms race, which swallowed so much of our wealth and presented so many dangers. We had to find a way out of the war in Afghanistan, so ruinous in terms of human lives, but also in terms of our image and our economy. Not to mention the faults of Brezhnevism. To carry out the necessary reforms required a new form of leadership and a lot of courage."

The direct speech and the energy brought by this new leader was a true break with the years of the gerontocracy that had gone before. And very soon, Gorbachev began to speak of reform. "When he became general secretary, he began to speak publicly about change, glasnost, openness, perestroika," said Roald Sagdeev. But if the new Soviet man appeared to be smiling publicly, managing affairs in the Kremlin, with the vast and complex bureaucracy of the Party, the military, and the KGB, was far from simple. "It started with a lot of daring," Sagdeev continued. "Then he thought he had to balance the conservatives, the old guard, and the younger reformers. He was straddling multiple chairs. And when the chairs separate, we fall. This is the best metaphor to use."

On his arrival, the Soviet people seemed to be won over immediately by the personality of the man they quickly dubbed "Gorby." "Many people were very enthusiastic, following him from the beginning," said Sagdeev.

But in two or three years, there was a lot of disappointment, and frustration began to build. Sagdeev, a plasma physicist who served as the general secretary's lead advisor for nuclear issues, decided that, "At first, Gorbachev spoke much. Then, he ended up listening too much to himself."

Inside the system, enthusiasm prevailed after Gorbachev's "election" as head of the Party. "The country was tired of those old leaders who kept on dying. But what kind of leader would it be? And what kind of leader did the country want?" asked Pavel Palazchenko, a young Foreign Ministry interpretor, who was about to become a close friend of Gorbachev. Gorbachev still occupies a large, but austere, office in the Kremlin.

"We had very few face-to-face meetings," says Roald Sagdeev. Except when Gorbachev was preparing for the summits with Reagan in Geneva, Reykjavík, and Washington. "We some-times had meetings in the Central Committee headquarters, with about twenty or thirty people. Above all, the advisers of the Soviet leader had to write report after report. I had to write a dozen on nuclear weapons issues. They had to be very detailed and I also offered my advice."

Gorbachev soon realized the system was no longer func-tioning as before. "People's loyalty could no longer be won by referring to the October Revolution or to the World War," he wrote in 1995, "but by an effective policy guaranteeing democ-racy, civil rights and a high standard of living. I was convinced that such a transfiguration of the CPSU was possible. But what did my comrades think of the leadership of the Party? The lead-ership of the country was at that time clearly divided. On the one hand, the real power moved from the Central Committee of the party to the person of the general secretary. In other words, the leading group saw its influence diminish in favor of the number one—Gorbachev."

On the other hand, the gap between conservatives and reformers widened considerably. "Even if there was not yet a cleavage or open controversy within the leadership," said Sagdeev, "a right wing and a left wing were emerging." Some saw elections as a victory for democracy, others as a defeat for the party. It was with this Soviet Union in the midst of internal political turmoil and in economic difficulty, led by this individual, that the Americans began preparing to renew a dialogue. In a word, a plunge into the unknown.

# THREE

# First Meeting in Geneva

T he hour has finally arrived. The first summit between Ronald Reagan and Mikhail Gorbachev is scheduled for November 19, 1985, on neutral ground in Geneva, Switzerland. Privately, the two leaders expressed their impatience to meet and see what could be negotiated by the two superpowers. The last summit between US and Soviet leaders was in June 1979 when Jimmy Carter and Leonid Brezhnev signed the SALT II treaty in Vienna. For six years, there had been no meeting between Americans and Soviets at the highest level. But discussions were far from broken off at other levels.

Foreign ministers and diplomatic and military advisers maintained regular contact throughout.

## The Leaders

On both sides, preparation embodies concentration, even a certain feverishness. "Gorbachev was very impatient," says Roald Sagdeev. "The team of advisers, of which I was a member, was sent to Geneva two weeks before. The idea was to acclimatize us, and to begin to discuss with our American counterparts. In two weeks, I had to give about forty interviews to American and European media. It was a sign that curiosity was at its height." That said, on the Soviet side, "we were not expecting anything special from these meetings," the nuclear adviser continues. "It was important for the two leaders to meet, nevertheless."

In the White House, the pace is no less feverish. "The president was very anxious to meet Gorbachev," says Patrick Buchanan, then director of communications at the White House. For four years Reagan had been trying to see Soviet leaders. Brezhnev, Andropov, and then Chernenko were old and died in rapid succession. Reagan followed Gorbachev's ascent with interest and hope. "He was happy," Buchanan continues. "So as soon as he took power, they agreed to meet in Geneva, where I was present."

The first meeting takes place on the morning of November 19 at the Maison Fleur d'Eau, an elegant building on the shores of

Lake Geneva. The weather is grayish, so the two leaders arrive wrapped in long coats. A fire is lit in the fireplace of the main salon, lined with brown wall-hangings. Reagan and Gorbachev settle down while the press photographers go to work. The first session begins. It is 10:20 A.M.

President Reagan begins the conversation by telling the general secretary that they can really talk now. The American then continues to explore the range of emotions he's feeling, reminding his Russian counterpart that he, too, comes from a rural background. He quickly paints the portrait of the two superpowers, believing they are the "only countries on Earth capable of triggering a Third World War, but also the only ones with the ability to bring peace to the world."

Gorbachev says he was approaching this meeting with great emotion and hoped that they would both realize the importance of this unique situation. For his part, Gorbachev thanks Reagan and stresses that "this meeting is profoundly important." The Soviet leader had received a delegation of American congressmen and Reagan administration advisors, but "he recognized the importance of a meeting with the president and the opportunity to speak quietly, with respect to the United States and directly to the president, on a broad range of issues."

This first dialogue lasts just over an hour—a real face to face, without advisers. The two men are accompanied only by their respective interpreters, since neither Reagan nor Gorbachev speaks the other's language. The two are then joined for forty-five minutes of discussion on the American side by Secretary of State George Shultz, chief of staff Donald Regan, US ambassador to Moscow Arthur Hartman, Rozanne Ridgway, Shultz's assistant on European affairs, and Mark Palmer, an American diplomat. On the Soviet side are Edouard Shevardnadze, minister of foreign affairs, Anatoli Dobrynin, ambassador to Washington, and three other counselors.

## Afghanistan on the Table

After a lunch break, delegations meet to discuss the first hot issues. For years, there would be several recurring themes between the two powers: nuclear weapons, of course, but also Afghanistan, the economy and international trade, and human rights abuses—all of central importance to the Reagan administration. Each time, it would be necessary to mix—and untangle—the files. Each could serve as a lever for negotiating an agreement on another issue.

The two sides meet at 2:30 P.M. Reagan, who is the official host on the first day, offers a brief welcome to Gorbachev. Then it's the Russian's turn. "The Soviets reject America's approach to the world around us," Gorbachev begins. "As if there was a plan of supremacy or Soviet domination. We have talked about this on a number of occasions. And when it creates regional problems, the US often accuses the Soviet Union of expansionism—in Afghanistan, Angola, or even in South Yemen." The general secretary warns that his country was not prepared to share the American point of view on the causes of regional conflicts. In a word, he accuses the Americans of having a biased view and calls for respect for the Soviet perspective. "You overestimate the power of the USSR," Gorbachev concludes.

The Soviet leader continues to speak without interruption. He mentions successively Afghanistan, Ethiopia, and the Third World more broadly. On Afghanistan, he argues that the USSR wants a "process of regularization, a political agreement under the aegis of the United Nations" and that the United States "could help." He then offers a package "involving a non-aligned Afghanistan, withdrawal of Soviet troops, return of refugees and international guarantees of non-interference." He adds that there was a possibility of "political reconciliation" in the region of Afghanistan.

## Strategic Arms

Gorbachev continues his discourse. The Americans, politely, do not interrupt him. He touches at length on the question of strategic armaments—that is, nuclear missiles. In short, he wants parity and opposes SDI (Strategic Defense Initiative), the infamous "Star Wars" antimissile system proposed by Reagan. After expressing his point of view with passion, it's the turn of the American president to respond.

Gorbachev's presentation, Reagan begins, "illustrates the lack of trust between us. It's difficult for us to comprehend the level of suspicion that the Soviet Union feels. It goes back to the time of the Second World War. Even when we were allies, you were suspicious of us. For example, you did not give permission for American bombers to land on Soviet soil to bomb our common enemy" Nazi Germany.

Reagan then addresses the issue of strategic weapons, defending SDI and accusing the USSR of having "added 6,000 nuclear warheads" since the signing of the SALT treaty, and 3,850 since SALT II went into effect. As for Afghanistan, Ronald Reagan accuses the Soviets of being responsible for the three million refugees who have fled the country, and for placing a puppet as that nation's ruler. The American president then unfolds all the regions where tension is rampant due to East-West conflict. These cold-war flash points include Cambodia, Laos and Vietnam, and several countries in Central America, particularly Nicaragua. "The Soviets have advisors there. The Sandinistas have built an incredible military machine, much more than necessary," the President charges.

At 3:40 P.M., Reagan proposes a stroll through the surrounding park before resuming their tête-à-tête. During this short walk, the two men talk about Reagan's acting career. "Tell Arbatov that I did not do anything other than B-series films," Reagan smiled, referring to Gorbachev's senior advisor on North American affairs, who had apparently immersed himself in Reagan's acting career. "Though I have also made some good ones." The Kremlin chief replies that he had recently seen *Kings*

*Row* and "very much appreciated it." His remark, perhaps even sincere, has its intended effect, flattering Reagan. The two men seem to appreciate each other.

This will turn out to be the only moment of relaxation between the two men. The second tête-à-tête takes place in the guest house, near the swimming pool. Again, the two leaders are alone with their interpreters. Then, in the evening, a dinner is organized at the invitation of the Gorbachevs, in the building of the Soviet mission in Geneva. The two first ladies are present, as are the foreign ministers. Political talk is shelved. The conversation is lighter. Nancy Reagan asks the Gorbachevs about the most interesting tourist sites in the Soviet Union. When caviar is served, "President Reagan talks about sturgeons in the Sacramento River and Gorbachev talks about hydroelectric power on the Volga," says the white paper produced later by the White House. The dinner continues with discussions of Tennessee Williams ("very popular in the Soviet Union"), and actress Elizabeth Taylor.

The ambiance is warm and pleasant. As proof, in a small departure from protocol, Gorbachev rises and blurts out an impromptu toast. Warmly, he "wishes to thank and welcome the President and Nancy. As I speak from the heart, I am pleased to be able to know our guests and I hope that it will be possible to arrive at a form of understanding that will enable us to discuss the problems of our people."

Reagan rises in turn. He thanks his hosts and embarks on a philosophical, even spiritual, speech. "I told Minister

Shevardnadze earlier that if men discovered that extraterrestrials were about to attack the Earth from Halley's comet, that would unite all the peoples of the world." Reagan then quotes a passage from the Acts of the Apostles, suggesting "we are all of the same blood, wherever we live on earth." Which nicely sets up the final act of the summit the next morning.

## Reagan Attacks on Human Rights

The Geneva Summit ends the following morning, November 20, 1985. A final one-on-one meeting takes place at the Soviet mission between 10:15 A.M. and 11:25 A.M. Back to the serious. Reagan wants to talk about "something the Soviets believe, erroneously, is a violation of their internal affairs." That is, human rights. More specifically, the law of "religious groups." In fact, the American president apologizes for the democratic system of his country, explaining to his counterpart that he "does not decide alone" on issues like this, and that Congress has a say, being "under the influence of religious groups and their lobbyists." He then mentions the celebration in the United States of St. Patrick's Day—a Catholic holiday. He also cites "Soviet peoples," namely "Ukrainian-Americans, Lithuanian-Americans, and Polish-Americans, each of whom has their organizations, customs and festivals." He also mentions the American Jewish community. In short, the message is clear: the United States disapproves of the oppression of religious freedom in the Soviet Union.

Gorbachev responds point by point. He refers first to "the use of human rights for political purposes," and observes he "does not understand that."

"In all sincerity, we are in favor of more exchanges with the United States—scientists, cultural representatives, all types of people," he says. "We two countries depend on one another in the world of today and tomorrow." He then mentions the increase in mixed marriages of Americans and Russians—more than four hundred in the last five years. He winds up turning to the question of Jews. "Their fate is also a concern of the Soviet government," he says. The crucial point on this issue is the families separated since the end of the Second World War. And Gorbachev promises to "examine this issue closely, case by case, humanely. But not when it is a political issue." The meeting ends with a belief that it is important that the two leaders have gotten to "know each other." Still, no agreement or draft agreement emerges from the Geneva Summit.

Behind the scenes, feelings are less diplomatic. Roald Sagdeev, a member of the delegation, says that "Geneva was just to get to know each other. After the first meeting, on the morning of the nineteenth, Gorbachev invited some people into the room: Abrameev, Shevardnadze, Primakov, Arbatov, and myself. There he gave us his first impressions. He was very disappointed, and I think I know why."

Savoring the impact of his words, Sagdeev continues, "In the USSR, as soon as he spoke, everyone had always been in awe.

Gorbachev was not prepared for anyone to behave like this. So I said, 'Mikhail Sergeyevich, you have to be prepared. If you quote Eisenhower on the military-industrial complex, Reagan is going to tell you that it was a joke. An American journalist who accompanied George Shultz on a plane back from the summit reported that he said in an interview, 'The Soviets are very naive and have a strange view of Reagan's reference to Eisenhower.'"

"What happened next, Gorbachev found most annoying," Sagdeev continues. "When Reagan wanted to change the conversation, he would take out a little card and read a quote from Lenin or Khrushchev, like 'We will bury you.' Was this a provocation on the part of Reagan, or awkwardness? Who knows? Reagan was very special, you know. They had to find a way to talk to each other. Gorbachev asked us, 'What should I do?' Shevardnadze, very intelligent, very wise, said: 'We are going to prepare cards for you with Eisenhower quotes.' And he was serious." Sagdeev dissolves in laughter.

Overall, the Americans saw the Geneva Summit as a fresh start—both countries "moving in the right direction." While no agreement was reached, particularly because of the difference in vision on the SDI program, the two sides agreed to meet at least twice in the near future. Once in Washington, then in Moscow.

Looking back, Gorbachev later wrote that he saw Geneva as a first step. "Our dialogue, intense and substantive, was even, at times, full of emotion. From the beginning, we were both frank, but Reagan became friendlier as we began to get to know each other better. Passions were still unleashed when we tackled human rights issues, regional conflicts or the Star Wars program, but by the end of the summit, I had finally convinced myself that Reagan was a man with whom one could work."

In the end, Geneva left a strange impression on the Soviets. "We were disappointed," says Sagdeev. "But Reagan and Gorbachev agreed to meet again. So, we forgot our disappointment once we got back to Moscow. What proposals could we put on the table next time? What could we expect from the Americans? This preparatory process was very interesting."

But the coming year, 1986, would prove critical with respect to nuclear weapons—alternating sharply between tensions, hopes, disappointment, and turns at the poker table.

# FOUR

# The Nuclear Question

At the moment in 1985 when Ronald Reagan was beginning his second term and Mikhail Gorbachev was taking over leadership of the Soviet Union, the two superpowers were still staring each other down, each daring the other to blink. The Cold War had been continuing without a pause since the end of the Second World War, particularly since the breakup of Germany into two countries in 1949: the Federal Republic of Germany, or West Germany, firmly glued to the Western Bloc, and the German Democratic Republic (GDR), in the unyielding grip of the Kremlin. The establishment in 1949 of two military alliances—NATO (the North Atlantic Treaty

Organization) on the one hand and the Warsaw Pact on the other—only cemented the status quo in Europe. Two crises in Berlin—the Berlin airlift of 1948 when the Soviet Union sought to strangle East Berlin by cutting off all road access, and then the Berlin Crisis that started in 1958 and ended in 1961 with the construction of the Berlin Wall and an end to free movement between East and West Berlin, only added to East-West tensions. Finally, the Cuban Missile Crisis in October 1962, when Nikita Khrushchev sought to install nuclear-armed missiles just 90 miles from the American coast, came within hours of hurtling the world into a third world war.

Other pressure points of the Cold War had led to two bloody regional conflicts—the Korean War (1950–1953) and the Vietnam War (1964–1973). In Latin America, in the 1970s and 1980s, the United States funded and supported anti-Communist factions or governments, their opponents receiving aid from Moscow. But neither the United States nor the Soviet Union ever attacked each other directly. The Cold War, with its multiple origins and points of contact, would never turn hot, or at least never "go nuclear."

Still, in the 1970s, Washington and Moscow agreed to halt the nuclear arms race in an effort to at least freeze the growth of arsenals that were more than sufficient to wipe out life on Earth many times over. Three basic texts were signed, one following the other. It's critical to explore their historical significance to understand the context of future events from the Reykjavík

Summit to the fall of the Soviet Union in which it may have played a not insignificant role.

The first treaty to be signed was called SALT I (Strategic Arms Limitation Treaty), or the "SALT Intermediate Agreement." It was an agreement between the USSR and the United States "limiting the number of strategic ballistic missiles that could be deployed by the two countries" and was signed in Moscow on May 26, 1972, by Leonid Brezhnev and Richard Nixon, then ratified by both nations. It entered into force on October 3, 1972. This agreement mandated a five-year freeze on the total number of ground-based intercontinental ballistic missiles, meaning that the two countries could not increase the number of launch devices beyond the number already operational or under construction. The number of missiles installed on submarines was restricted to 800 for each side, divided between fifty submarines.

## Next Step? An ABM Treaty

In this type of agreement, the verification measures are paramount—ensuring that the opponent follows the rules of the game and keeps his word, or in the language of the treaty, "Compliance with the provisions of the Agreement shall be verified by national technical means, and matters relating to the implementation of the Agreement shall be dealt with by the Permanent Consultative Commission established by the Treaty on the Limitation of Antiballistic Missile Systems (ABM Treaty)."

The ABM Treaty was a key to every arms agreement that followed. Also signed by the two major powers in 1972, the text "prohibits deploying a system to defend the national territory against a strategic ballistic missile attack." Meaning, in conventional language—you can't remove from your opponent the possibility of destroying you if he strikes first. In the Cold War, this concept became enshrined in the term "Mutually Assured Destruction" or MAD—the philosophy that secured both superpowers and the rest of the world from nuclear holocaust.

The treaty stipulates that the two signatory states must review the provisions of the agreement every five years. It also establishes a Permanent Consultative Commission, which must meet at least twice a year. Without this treaty's ban on creating defensive devices, the development of ever more efficient and potent offensive weapons to counteract them would inevitably result in continued escalations of the arms race.

But in 1974, the Soviet Union and the United States adopted a protocol amending the treaty. The new text, authorized "a deployment area of ballistic missile systems (ABM) to protect either the national capital or an intercontinental ballistic missile deployment area (ICBM)." The Soviets quite reasonably chose to protect their capital, Moscow. The Americans began deploying the Safeguard system to defend Grand Forks, North Dakota, a remote nuclear missile launch site.

Discussions to extend the SALT I treaty, which had only been expected to last five years, began in 1977, assembling military, scientific and diplomatic specialists from both countries. The talks culminated in Leonid Brezhnev and Jimmy Carter signing the SALT II Treaty on June 18, 1979, in Vienna. This text would wind up never being ratified by the US Senate, but the two countries nevertheless respected the provisions of the treaty, which was to remain in force until December 31, 1985.

**State of Forces**

In the mid-1980s, technological advances made it possible to build a broad range of missiles capable of carrying multiple nuclear warheads: intercontinental ballistic missiles (ICBMs), with a range of over 6,000 miles and thus able to span continents, and the more limited intermediate range missiles (IRBMs). The discussions that began in Geneva in 1985 between the two superpowers were aimed at achieving a nuclear weapons reduction treaty—not simply a freeze at current levels, but an actual removal of a reciprocal number of missiles and their warheads. In a now declassified top secret internal White House document from the time, we find a summary of the positions of both sides and especially the order of magnitudes of the various nuclear missiles deployed. Such data is among the ultimate secrets of national defense, but was disclosed to each other in the course of these early talks. Eventually, the two countries agreed to limit nuclear warheads to 7,500 for the United States and 8,000 for the USSR (the difference based on the inclusion or exclusion of certain categories of weapons). There are 1,600 missile-launch vehicles on both sides, each capable of carrying multiple warheads.

For intermediate-range missiles, the agreement called for limiting their number to 100 in Europe for each of the parties; the Soviet SS-20 deployed in Asia was separate from the number of intermediate negotiations. This represented a truly dramatic reduction, since each side had at least 2,690 weapons in Europe when the talks got underway. Another document, dated October 1986, spelled out the forces the Soviets had deployed: one page on "Warsaw Pact missiles and tactical rockets," details the Scud, Russian Spider, and Scaleboard families of missiles, with supporting drawings. The SS-12s have a range of 515 miles. The SS-20 and SS-21, operational since 1981, have a range of less than 65 miles, but have been deployed in East European satellite countries, directly threatening Western Europe. This is why the Americans responded with the installation of Pershing II missiles in West Germany, a move made possible by the approval of the British and the support of French president François Mitterrand in 1982, a sharp reversal of policies that had prevailed since Charles de Gaulle removed France from NATO's military arm. All four countries—Britain, France, the United States, and Russia—controlled, as part of the treaty ending World War II, the nature of arms deployed in Germany, whose military was in theory controlled by the four Allied occupying powers.

## The Shock of SDI

These nearly identical nuclear forces reached a record level in the 1980s. Having increased their destructive capacity over the previous decade, the two superpowers, under Leonid Brezhnev and Richard Nixon, and then Brezhnev and Jimmy Carter, felt it was essential to put a brake on this plunge toward Armageddon. A moral conscience? An economic imperative? Or simply self-preservation in the interest of a horrific accident? Inevitably, SALT I, then SALT II germinated in the best minds on both sides simultaneously.

When Ronald Reagan entered into world politics, this precarious balance began experiencing an unexpected upheaval that threatened to upend the entire concept of MAD on which it was based. Ronald Reagan's announcement of a space defense program suddenly risked transforming the balance between the superpowers for years, perhaps generations, to come—even irreversibly. Ronald Reagan had already spoken publicly, even before becoming president, of his fear of destruction of the planet due to a nuclear war. This nightmare seemed to obsess him.

So Reagan threw down the gauntlet on March 23, 1983. That night, in a prime time nationally televised address from the Oval Office, Ronald Reagan talked with his fellow Americans about "peace and national defense." Dressed in a navy-blue suit and a red tie with white patterns, he looked into the camera in front of him, the lens framed by a teleprompter, even though the president was holding his speech in his hands. It lasted nearly half an hour. Like a teacher, Reagan launched into his explanation with the conviction of the "great communicator" at the peak of his game.

In that prime-time speech, Reagan announced the SDI program to the United States and the world—the Strategic Defense Initiative. It would quickly be dubbed "Star Wars," a reference to the cinematic saga of George Lucas, whose third installment, *Return of the Jedi,* had just taken the world by storm. "If we, the people, could live with the knowledge that our security does not rest in our ability to counter-attack a Soviet attack, but to intercept and destroy intercontinental ballistic missiles even before they reach our own soil or that of our allies?" He let that question hang, the answer clear and straightforward. The president concluded by calling on the "scientific community" to help him reach this goal, that was still no more than a pipe dream and an admittedly most loaded phrase.

In the months that followed, the top officials of the Reagan administration went to great lengths to "sell" this decision to the public and to America's allies, often with limited success. In an internal memo prepared by Bob Linhard to Robert McFarlane, the national security advisor, dated April 15, 1985, the urgency had clearly become palpable. Barely months before the first summit with Gorbachev, the White House was still scrambling to find the best arguments to sell SDI. The message boiled down to vocabulary—elements of language, choosing the best and most effective phrase to dramatize a concept that did not yet even exist, had been neither tested or deployed, and that few believed really could. In his memo, Linhard appeared most concerned with "providing terms of reference," as well as "a path regarding technological demonstrations" of the scheme, while stressing the "transient" aspect of these studies, still ill-defined even in an experimental context.

One text prepared for the president, emphasized so "crucial [was it] to maximize the support of the public, Congress and our allies that our presentations of the nature and goals of the SDI program must be coherent and accurate." The text then focused on a crucial point: "This support rests largely on our ability to emphasize compatibility with the ABM Treaty and [the fact that this program] is comparable to the research that the Soviets have been conducting for many years." Indeed, the ABM Treaty prevents any deployment of antimissile systems. Apparently, messages from the government had been somewhat chaotic since the president's March televised speech. "Unfortunately, we have not spoken with one voice," the document continued, referring to "confusion and fuzzy statements, thereby creating suspicion about our intentions." Several such points are underlined. The press and the public would eventually find these very arguments in the documents published by the government a few weeks later in the ongoing attempt to win public support.

First point: "Research will last several years. We intend to abide strictly by the limits imposed by the ABM Treaty and we expect the same from the Soviets."

Second point: "We do not know where the research will lead. We will develop and deploy only if the research indicates [that it is possible]."

Third point: "We will judge whether defenses are desirable only if they can last and the cost stays within bounds."

Fourth point: "If these criteria are met, we will want to consult the Soviets about how to amend the ABM Treaty."

Fifth, and most critical point: "The objective of SDI is strategic balance and better deterrence, not superiority." Reagan needed to persuade his own people, but also Mikhail Gorbachev that his intent was honorable and above all defensive, not in any sense offensive.

If the Reagan administration was finding such difficulty explaining the nature and intent of this program, it was for quite a simple reason—doubt. Was SDI ever intended to be a purely defensive program? Or was it simply a vehicle for moving the arms race into space? For in the end, fear was spreading rapidly that, thanks to their scientific and technological advances, the Americans would be in a position within a few years to deploy a space shield that would prevent Soviet missiles from landing on American or European soil. This would involve orbiting satellites, each carrying a laser beam sufficiently powerful and accurate to destroy an intercontinental missile launched and in full flight. It was then and remains today an ultimately fanciful concept.

## Global Reactions

The announcement of the SDI program received widespread reactions throughout the world including many of America's closest allies. After carefully weighing its options, France weighed in with a letter dated June 11, 1984, from the French ambassador to Washington reviewing "several issues of concern." In three densely typed pages, the position of the French government was laid out quite clearly. "Deterrence, which has played a vital role in maintaining peace in Europe, is based on maintaining an ability to respond in the event of an assault, no matter how technology changes. But France, like the international community as a whole, can only be concerned today when it sees the emergence of new technologies that can threaten stability—and thus peace—that has resulted, until now, from the presence of invulnerable means of nuclear response."

The diplomat, the official voice of the French presidency in Washington, puts it directly: "Far from promoting the reduction of offensive systems, the prospect of deploying new defensive systems will only have the opposite effect. Developing such a system is in itself an encouragement to relaunch the offensive arms race. Each power will seek to saturate the anti-ballistic systems provided by the other and to increase non-ballistic cruise missiles."

The fear of the international community was clearly and widely stated: While accepting that perhaps the Americans are sincere in their purely defensive objective, militarizing space is a bad idea and will only accelerate the arms race. And if inter-continental missiles disappear, nuclear missiles with short or intermediate range will quickly proliferate.

## The Soviets Respond

Following the Reagan speech in 1983, the Soviets decided simply to stay the course. The announcement of the concept of SDI, even if its development and its realization would be some years in the future, or never, was troubling. But Mikhail Gorbachev's nuclear adviser, Roald Sagdeev, said that Star Wars did not cause panic. "We must remember the general state of mind before Reagan's speech: after the Second World War, in the mid-1950s, there was a lot of debate about how to protect ourselves. Many thought that it was necessary to defend oneself with a civil defense. Dig deeply to protect ourselves!" He chuckled at this idea, then began again seriously: "Others were saying, 'Let's invent a defense system.' So there were a lot of ideas, including lasers, missile interceptors with nuclear particles. Everything was put on the table and a lot of money was spent on both sides."

At the same time, many American scientists were opposed to SDI, for the reason already mentioned by the French statement: "These defenses can only cause an arms race. For if one camp perceives that the other camp has succeeded in building such defenses, deterrence no longer works. So it would push them to build a more important attack system. This dynamic offense against defense would only cause a new arms race."

Sagdeev then described the opening of a "non-governmental channel," a parallel diplomacy, quietly initiated by both governments, that continued through the remainder of the Cold War—but only on the scientific level officially. "With international scientists, we met at the Pugwash conferences. Even Einstein was a part of this mechanism at one time. The meetings took place through our national academies of science, respectively Soviet and American. Finally, through the Committees on International Security and Arms Control (CISAC)."

For Sagdeev, the ABM Treaty and the SALT treaties have been critical. "The idea was that defense was dangerous and that nuclear missiles should be limited. The only thing that worried us, in 1982," he continued, referring to the Soviet position, "was not defense and SDI, but anti-satellite weapons. It was a dangerous development because the stability and balance of the Cold War was maintained by both sides through their ability to spy from space. If we started to destroy or blind these satellites, it would create a lot of suspicion."

It was in this context, according to Roald Sagdeev, that Reagan's initiative appeared. "Out of nowhere," Sagdeev confesses with the same astonishment, more than thirty years later. "In the early 1980s, we began to think about a treaty that would limit defenses in space. Moreover, in March 1983, I was in Washington with a group of Russian scientists to meet with some American counterparts, to speak specifically about our fears about anti-satellite weapons. We were en route to the airport to return to Moscow when we learned from a newspaper that Reagan had made his speech about Star Wars. It came out of nowhere, for us. And not only for us! Even for our American scientist colleagues."

The reaction of these scientists, each specialists in nuclear issues and seasoned political negotiators, was impulsive: "Is this guy crazy?" Sagdeev asked again today about Ronald Reagan in 1983. "The discussions also focused on the technical feasibility of this program: lasers? X-rays? etc."

That said, the naiveté of the Soviets must be taken in hindsight with some skepticism. Did the USSR not also have the technological capacity to create its own SDI? Had the equivalent of Star Wars at one time or another not been at least in the head of an official of the Kremlin? Roald Sagdeev is categorical. Yes, it was certainly envisaged—but promptly abandoned. "There had been several attempts on the part of military manufacturers—too ambitious," he said. One of these ideas was very similar to SDI, with small interceptor missiles in orbit, in space. Still, this was rejected. At least, on our side, we understood that it would never work." According to Sagdeev, these studies took place in 1976 and 1977. No later.

In Washington, though, in the wake of Reagan's address, the concept, if not the reality, of SDI began to take shape. If the American scientific community did not conceal its skepticism, or even its hostility to the program when it was announced, the politicians seem convinced. Certainly, the Republicans. "I was very supportive of SDI," said Patrick Buchanan, who was a journalist before being hired as the White House director of communications for Ronald Reagan's second term and member of the National Security Council, and eventually an unsuccessful presidential candidate. "In Washington DC, some thought it was just a balloon that was going to deflate, that it could never be realized. But, clearly, the Soviets were impressed."

John Poindexter, who became Reagan's national security advisor in 1985, also recalls his commitment to Star Wars. For this career admiral, it's necessary to strike any adversary hard. He even claims a share of the paternity of the project. "Towards the end of 1982, I was still a military assistant at the White House. I went to [National Security Advisor Robert] McFarlane and explained that I wanted to set up a small study group on 'strategic defense.' We were then in the weeks leading up to Ronald Reagan's announcement on television. We delivered our findings to the president in February 1983. He first presented SDI's research and development to a panel of prominent figures in the East Room. I was disappointed, because most people were too politically correct and seemed already to decree that it would not be technologically possible," smiles John Poindexter today. "Now, this is not the scientific method. You must have an hypothesis, then experiment and see if this hypothesis is correct. In short, I was disappointed by the scientific community."

Never mind. The Star Wars concept would have its moment in the sun. In any case, this is what the president's closest advisors thought, as well as the president himself. The pressure was turned on. And the very existence of this project had the effect of providing more leverage for the United States in the bilateral discussions with the Soviets. For Patrick Buchanan, "the Soviets saw SDI as a major threat. They had invested a huge part of their national wealth in their SS-19, SS-18, SS-24 ballistic missile programs. All these weapons! So I think they saw it as a neutralizer of their long-term strategic arsenal. This is what brought Gorbachev to Reykjavík."

The urgency to negotiate a reduction of nuclear weapons was building sharply, at least on the Soviet side. So, as Buchanan observes, Mikhail Gorbachev would try to speed up the calendar. Even if that meant forcing the destiny of the world.

# FIVE

# *Reykjavík: The Preparations*

A letter. This is how the general secretary of the Communist Party of the Soviet Union chose to address the president of the United States. In four dense pages, written on September 15, 1986, the leader of the Eastern bloc offered his inventory of strategic forces, the geopolitical situation, and concluded with a request for an appointment with his American counterpart, a tête-à-tête, "perhaps on a single day, in Iceland or in London." Gorbachev wanted a "frank, confidential and private discussion," raising the possibility of "drafting a draft agreement on two or three very specific questions that you and I could sign during my [future] visit to the United States."

## Genesis of a Meeting

Such a session began to take shape in the summer of 1986, mainly on the Soviet side. In Washington, the Geneva post-summit meetings were continuing, but it was indeed Mikhail Gorbachev who was already contemplating an approach for a new meeting between the two men. In his memoirs, Anatoly Chernyaev, Gorbachev's main diplomatic adviser beginning in 1985, recalls how the Soviet leader made his decision to organize a new informal summit with Reagan. "One of the major events was François Mitterrand's visit to Moscow," he wrote. Mitterrand, who had just returned from the United States, observed, "In my conversations with the Americans, I asked very directly what they really wanted. Was it in their interest for the USSR to spend more on their economic development by reducing their military budget? Or, on the contrary, do they want to exhaust the USSR through the arms race, divert it from its history and force Soviet leaders to spend more and more indiscriminately on their army? I told Reagan that the first choice is peace, that the second is war."

"Of course, Gorbachev was fully in agreement with this," said Chernyaev. Then Mitterrand added, "Unlike many of his predecessors, Reagan is not an automaton. He's a human being."

On July 18, Gorbachev met former president Richard Nixon, who was visiting Moscow. Nixon, the leader who reopened relations with Mao Zedong and China, and the cosigner of the

SALT I treaty with Leonid Brezhnev, had some useful insights for Gorbachev. "You have correctly noticed President Reagan's popularity with the Americans," Nixon told Gorbachev. "I have known President Reagan for a long time, almost thirty years. And I have the strong impression that he regards US-Soviet relations as his personal responsibility. He was very impressed by your conversation, as well as your personal commitment to the cause of peace between our two countries. He also thinks he has established a personal relationship with you and, based on that, he thinks agreement is possible if you work together." To which Gorbachev replied: "You can rest assured that [I] have no diabolical purpose, [that I am] not trying to win a diplomatic game. Such an approach would make no sense. We want to find a path to friendship between our countries."

The conversations with Mitterrand and Nixon weighed heavily on Gorbachev. So it was during a few days of vacation in a house in Crimea, on the shores of the Black Sea, that the idea of the letter to Ronald Reagan began germinating in Gorbachev's mind. Rather than surrounding himself with his usual counselors, the Soviet leader invited only Anatoly Chernyaev, who joined the Soviet leader daily before lunch on the veranda or in the office, for a review of current topics and coded cables. In his memoirs, Chernyaev recalls the morning Gorbachev received a draft letter from Anatoly Kovalev, then an aide to Foreign Minister Eduard Shevardnadze. After reading it, he blurted out, "This is nonsense." But he immediately began to think aloud and told Chernyaev to send a dispatch: "Emergency: Prepare a draft of a letter to the president of the United States. Suggest a meeting in late September or early October, either in London or . . ." He paused for a few moments, then continued, ". . . in Reykjavík."

Chernyaev looked at him in surprise. "Why Reykjavík?" Gorbachev replied, "It's a good idea. Halfway between us and them, and none of the great powers will be upset."

## The Chernobyl Shock

Beyond the context of the bilateral discussions on nuclear weapons, which would justify the Reykjavík Summit, the first half of 1986 was marked by two events that directly affected the two superpowers. On Saturday, April 26, 1986, reactor number 4 of the Chernobyl nuclear power plant in the Ukrainian Soviet Republic melted down. The resulting radioactive cloud began drifting north and west further into Europe before dissipating, sending chills across the continent and around the world. It remains today the most serious nuclear accident in history. This industrial earthquake, with disastrous ecological consequences, immediately began raising deep concerns at the highest political levels on the planet. Moscow, embarrassed internationally, was forced to react.

This reaction, however, was delayed by the all-but-paralyzed Soviet bureaucracy, much to the chagrin, bordering on rage, of Mikhail Gorbachev. "The accident that occurred . . . constituted the most spectacular and terrible proof of the decay of our equipment and the exhaustion of the possibilities of an old and outmoded system," Gorbachev later recalled. "At the same time, and this is the paradox of history, this incident seriously affected a host of reforms that were underway, totally disorienting the country. During the first few days, for want of complete information, we felt intuitively that the problems had taken on a dramatic dimension and that the consequences could be very serious."

Beyond the internal consequences of the Chernobyl accident for Ukraine and the rest of the Soviet Union, Gorbachev observed there were substantial international repercussions. "The Cold War played an aggravating role because of the secrecy between the two military blocs, even in the field of civilian nuclear energy," he said, pointing to the "blissful optimism," of the supposed perfection of civilian nuclear technology.

Still, it was not until May 14, 1986, more than two weeks after the tragedy, that Gorbachev was in a position to make a public, televised statement. With a sober "Good evening, comrades," the general secretary of the Communist Party began his address to his fellow citizens. "As you all know, bad luck befell us—the accident at the Chernobyl nuclear power plant. This deeply affected the Soviet people and worried the international public." Gorbachev continued, providing details of the accident, without concealing the seriousness of the accident. He also thanked the Eastern European countries for their help, even commending two American doctors. But then he veered off onto a succession of *ad hominem* attacks, singling out "some NATO countries, especially the United States, for carrying out an anti-Soviet campaign" to destabilize the Soviet Union with overly alarmist reports on the consequences of the accident. Which did little to improve the already strained relations between the two superpowers.

The United States promptly denied throwing oil on the fire. On the contrary, the Reagan administration refused to admit any interference in or criticism of Gorbachev's leadership. "President Reagan had asked us not to propagandize" the problem, wrote Jack Matlock, a member of the National Security Council, who would later become ambassador to Moscow. "He felt that we should dismiss all political considerations, try to help if necessary, inform our people of what we knew but avoid hysteria about the danger of nuclear power plants. He was for nuclear power plants, especially if they could be protected." Still, according to Matlock, the American-led task force held its first press conference on Chernobyl on April 30, several days before the Soviets themselves, which could not have produced a positive reaction in Moscow.

## The Daniloff Affair

The other defining moment was the Daniloff Affair and was quite another order of magnitude. No human or ecological catastrophe here, but a scandal ripped from the pages of an espionage novel that was destined to suddenly strain relations between the two superpowers.

The man had class. Tall, thin, with salt-and-pepper hair and black wire-rimmed spectacles, Nicholas Daniloff carried his fifty-one years well. This American journalist graduated from Harvard and was the correspondent in Moscow for the magazine *U.S. News & World Report*, America's third largest weekly after *Time* and *Newsweek*. His grandfather, Yuri Danilov, was chief of operations at the headquarters of the Russian Imperial Army during the First World War. Unsurprisingly, Nicholas spoke impeccable Russian and had managed to cultivate remarkable sources in the still tightly controlled Soviet Union. None of this, however, prevented Nicholas from being arrested by the KGB in Moscow on September 2, 1986. The given reason for his arrest, followed by imprisonment? Espionage. The real reason was that he was simply too good at his job. But according to the Soviet authorities, at the time he was seized, Daniloff had documents belonging to the Soviet government—a claim that the journalist and American authorities denied. Behind the Daniloff Affair, however lay a diplomatic settling of accounts. Three days before, the United States had arrested a certain Gennady Zakharov, an employee of the Soviet Mission to the United Nations in New York. And Zakharov was most definitely a spy.

Finally, after bitter behind-the-scenes negotiations, Daniloff was released on September 23, put on a plane for Frankfurt, Germany, and allowed to return to the United States. In exchange, Zakharov was released without being charged and deported to Moscow. A good faith transaction of sorts. At the last moment, however, in the middle of this acute crisis, a third name appeared—Yuri Orlov, a Soviet dissident, physicist, and human rights activist. Orlov had been sentenced to seven years in a labor camp in 1978 and then to five years of internal exile in Siberia for having founded a group to monitor the application of the Helsinki Accords human rights agreements by the USSR. After seven years in the Urals, he was sent to the Siberian village of Kobyai, where he lived in a barely insulated house without sanitary facilities. In the winter, it is sixty degrees below zero Fahrenheit. Orlov was finally allowed to emigrate to the West after the successful completion of negotiations on the Daniloff case.

These apparently superficial cases wound up poisoning a broad range of relations between the two countries. Whatever fragile confidence remained after the Geneva Summit of 1985 was again shaken. The Daniloff case revived the issue of human rights, but neither government appeared to be acting in especially good faith. In a memorandum to President Reagan, John Poindexter drew some important lessons from the Daniloff case: "I think that the way the Soviets handled Daniloff's arrest illustrates some important differences between American and Soviet psychologies, and national security. But this information was useful for our tactics in other negotiations with the Soviets."

Ronald Reagan took a small victory lap just before Reykjavík. The American president, unhappily, gave an impression to journalists that the Soviets blinked first in the spaghetti western-style duel of the Daniloff Affair. The next day, he walked back this statement, but the American press screamed victory and believed that it was indeed the United States that emerged the winner in this faceoff. Polling in the United States supported this impression. Some 52 percent of those interviewed by Gallup for *Newsweek* approved the release of Nicholas Daniloff and Gennady Zakharov, while 36 percent disapproved. Interestingly, 72 percent of Americans believed the two men had been "exchanged," while the White House went to great lengths to assert that was not the case—this affair involved two distinct and separate negotiations. As for the broader question of Cold War posturing, the responses were deeply reflective of American psychology during this late stage of the Cold War. Three-quarters of the respondents believed the Daniloff case "will allow the USSR to more easily accuse innocent Americans as soon as Soviet spies are arrested in the United States." Fifty-five percent also believed that it was the Americans who yielded to the Soviets in this case, but 70 percent agreed that "it was the best way to get Daniloff's release given the context."

## Preparations on the American Side

Despite this apparently toxic background, long before Gorbachev's letter to Reagan suggesting an informal meeting in Iceland, the Americans were actively preparing for Summit II—the second meeting at the highest level following Geneva in 1985. A March 27, 1986, document attests to some impatience within the White House. In this memorandum to Ronald Reagan via his chief of staff Donald Regan, counselor William Henkel listed the issues that needed to be addressed. "One of the results you achieved in 1985 was the Geneva Summit and the new beginning, a dialogue for peace that was so well received by the public," Henkel wrote to Reagan. "Geneva has given you an enormous boost on the issues of peace and the conduct of foreign policy. The most tangible result was your agreement with the General Secretary to plan two more summits."

The documents show that this second summit was to be held in the United States, but with a much broader mandate. The state visit of the Soviet leader was to echo the life of Ronald Reagan himself. In a July 14 memo, Henkel outlined a draft program of events for the visit. During the first two days, Reagan would welcome Gorbachev to Washington, with "substantive discussions held at the White House." On the third day of the visit, an "outside Washington event, accompanied by the President." But then, the Soviet leader would be offered a tour across the United States, for two days, without Ronald Reagan, who would join Gorbachev in Los Angeles on a fifth day with a lunch at the Reagan ranch outside Santa Barbara. The document mentions that

Gorbachev had expressed a wish to speak at the John F. Kennedy Presidential Library in Boston and pay a visit to Reagan's birthplace in Illinois.

Meanwhile, in Washington, Reagan's calendar was filling up. On September 30, he was booked to address officials of the World Bank and the International Monetary Fund. There followed bill signings and a meeting with congressional leaders on energy measures that Reagan was anxious to shepherd through. The receipt of the Gorbachev letter sent on September 15, however, upset all these schedules. Plans for an official summit in Washington were shelved, at least for the moment. With Reagan accepting Gorbachev's invitation, the priority turned to Reykjavík. The White House teams had to prepare in just a few weeks—in both form and substance.

## On the Menu for Reykjavík

Reagan's entourage was working one subject above all else— the size of the nuclear arsenal and the question of disarmament. The equilibrium of nuclear terror had remained unchanged since the previous summit in Geneva a year earlier, but the Chernobyl disaster and the settling of accounts around the Daniloff affair had strained relations between the two superpowers. In Washington, however, on the substance of nuclear issues, mistrust always prevailed as to the sincerity of the Soviets. Did they really want to disarm?

Were the internal reforms announced by Gorbachev not little more than a smoke screen?

Even before Geneva, a document issued by the Department of State on February 1, 1985, focused on Moscow's failure to honor a number of its signed commitments. The report included declassified portions of the president's report to Congress on the Defense Authorization Act, and observed that "the Government of the United States reaffirms the conclusions of January 1984 that the USSR violated the Final Act of the Helsinki Accords [dealing with human rights and European security], the protocol on chemical, biological and toxic weapons of the Geneva Convention and two provisions of SALT II: Telemetric Encryption and Modernization of Ballistic Missiles (ICBM)." The American accusation continued even more precisely that "the United States Government also reiterates that the USSR probably violated the prohibition on the deployment of SS-16 by the SALT II Treaty and the limit to nuclear tests laid down in the Threshold Test Ban Treaty. In addition, the U.S. Government has determined that the USSR has violated the ABM Treaty (through the installation, orientation and capabilities of the Krasnoyarsk radar), the Limited Test Ban Treaty, violated the SALT II provision which prohibits more than one new type of ICBM and probably violated the ABM Treaty by testing surface-to-air missiles." The document then details for two more pages, point by point, the alleged Soviet failures across the entire range of treaties between the two countries.

It was in this atmosphere of suspicion that the West Wing of the White House actively began its preparations for the meeting in Reykjavík. In the two weeks preceding the president's departure for Iceland—the Reykjavík Summit having been scheduled for October 11 and 12, 1986—internal meetings and notes began to proliferate. The pressure was rising. On September 30, a report by the State Department's "special mission team" identified issues to be discussed with the Soviets. This long document was addressed only to four people: three members of the National Security Council (Robert Pearson, Jack Matlock, Rodney McDaniel) and an undisclosed adviser to Vice President George H. W. Bush. Over five-and-a-half pages, the team of diplomats summarized the main themes to be discussed in the conversations between Reagan and Gorbachev.

"The meeting in Reykjavík is not a signing ceremony or a media event, but a preparatory pre-summit:

—no signature on any agreement is expected or necessary;

—the objective is to identify areas where progress is possible and to accelerate negotiations;

—the meeting in Iceland must prepare the ground for the visit of Gorbachev to the United States, and not replace it."

This last point was especially important for the Americans. Reykjavík must prepare for an official summit with great fanfare in Washington later in the year or the following year. This insistence was repeated in a host of White House documents. The task force summary continued, at times emphasizing key sentences, like this one: "We will not sacrifice American interests in order to have a summit or to obtain agreements. We will focus on a broad agenda that is essential for true peace and a more productive relationship, including human rights, arms reduction, regional issues and bilateral issues."

The team then reiterates that "the United States has made positive proposals in each of the areas." With regard to the theme "Successfully Reducing the Arsenal," the authors say: "As a priority: to reduce offensive nuclear weapons and to eliminate them in the long term; to move towards a safer world in which strategic defenses reinforce peace; reduce the imbalance in conventional armaments and limit the risk of war by accident or disagreement; and ban chemical and biological weapons worldwide."

The next page is devoted to "arguments." In telegraphic style, the report continues, "Private session, informal, to review the agenda of the visit of Secretary Gorbachev." Reykjavík would, in a sense, serve as a substitute for Gorbachev's visit to the United States, which Gorbachev proposed and the president agreed. The president also wanted to insist on a commitment to improve the broad spectrum of US-Soviet relations. There was a potential for progress. The meeting in Iceland could be an additional help. The Soviets would concentrate on arms control. The United States would insist on balancing and discussing a comprehensive agenda: arms reduction, human rights, regional conflicts, bilateral issues.

On October 3, the Reagan team finally moved into higher gear. This date seemed key to the White House. After having the conversations and writing the documents devoted to the president's objectives and intentions, it was now time to flesh out the concrete positions he should take. In a confidential document produced by the National Security Council and signed by Reagan, the working groups were assembled. A diagram attached to the document shows three levels of preparation for the summit. First, the Senior Planning Group, headed jointly by Chief of Staff Donald T. Regan and National Security Advisor John Poindexter who would "coordinate the preparation of the meetings."

Just below was the White House Working Group, led by Alton Keel, assistant to the president for national security affairs, and Dennis Thomas, another assistant to the president. This group was "responsible for coordination between the White House team and the National Security Council. Its members were senior advisers and NSC officers with direct responsibility for the preparation of the summit." Yet another level included the Senior Policy Committee, also headed by Alton Keel, "responsible for political initiatives," dealing with the substance of the files. This committee was supported by the Policy Support Group headed by Jack Matlock and the Arms Control Support Group, led by Bob Linhard, the arms control specialist closest to the president. For this group, the goal is "determining the appropriate policies" that should emerge from the summit—in short, to make proposals and establish negotiating scenarios.

Finally, this whole edifice is accompanied by an Operations Coordinating Committee, headed by NSC Soviet and European Affairs Officer Tyrus Cobb, flanked by Franklin Lavin, executive secretary of the NSC. They are the ones who would have to put oil in the gears to ensure "day-to-day coordination for the preparation of meetings and report" between each of the various working groups.

This architecture may seem intricate, but in reality it is the bare necessity to make the American presidency function in the complex scenarios of a strategic superpower summit. In all, very few people would be directly involved in the process—some fifteen advisers, responsible for preparing in record time crucial discussions for the future of the United States and the planet. Of course it must be remembered that these issues had been the subject of an ongoing dialogue at lower levels even before the Geneva Summit of 1985 and even more intensively after. But the acceleration of the schedule at the request of Gorbachev led to a sudden call to battle stations—effectively a bureaucratic commando operation so that the president could arrive combat-ready in Reykjavík.

The president himself became directly involved a few days after his support groups began their work. On October 6, he informally invited himself to a meeting of the NSC in the White House situation room. And Reagan made several comments to his present advisors. "I am very pleased to meet with you today." Reagan begins in his characteristic manner—folksy, yet all business. "It is a chance to say hello to all of you and to congratulate you for the work you are doing on defense and peace issues. Then, knowing your interest in the matter, I wanted to seize this opportunity to offer a perspective—the American perspective, if you will, on the meetings between Mr. Gorbachev and myself later this week in Reykjavík. Recently, as you know, there has been speculation about the signing of an important disarmament agreement between the United States and the Soviet Union. This kind of rumor is not surprising when the leaders of our two countries meet. There are always those who predict treaties and historical breakthroughs. Yet, when this kind of speculation happens, I cannot help but think back to the first administrative post I occupied. I hope you will forgive me for dredging up this memory, but as a union president, I spent a lot of time at the negotiating table and learned a valuable lesson. In this, the initial phase of negotiations, lay the foundation, refine the program, establish areas of agreement and disagreement—and who pays in the end.

"From the beginning, we have tried to make this a historic moment of this presidency. We have tried to maintain a cautious, realistic and deliberate approach to US-Soviet relations. Instead of rushing into negotiations with the Soviets that were ill-prepared, this administration has taken its time from the earliest days to clarify the essential elements of foreign policy: our commitment to the twin goals of world peace and freedom; the desire to be realistic and frank towards the Soviets; to publicly define the crucial; moral distinction between totalitarianism and democracy and to actively help those who struggle for their own self-determination."

After these general remarks, the president turned to the Daniloff affair, which had just been resolved. He highlighted the difficulty of getting along with the Soviets, his own personal difficulties with trusting them. He then reviewed the issues of regional conflicts, particularly Afghanistan, still occupied by the USSR. Reagan ends his impromptu speech in front of his advisors with the issue of disarmament, which will be at the center of the Reykjavík talks: "We believe that this summit can be useful in preventing war as we move towards a world with more personal freedoms and respect for human rights. We believe that the summit program reflects the positive changes that have taken place in the world. We are not talking only about arms control, but weapons, as well as human rights and regional conflicts. Progress toward our goals of peace and freedom will not be easy. As I said in my Saturday radio address, we need the support of all Americans. We need your help. And we also need careful preparation. And that is why we have accepted these discussions in Iceland and we are looking forward to meeting Mr. Gorbachev there. And that's why, since I think about it, I have to go back and do my homework and read my files."

This type of impromptu meeting between the president and his men was not a frequent occasion. Reagan's agenda was minutely crafted. The fact that he went to the meeting to give his frank impressions to his advisers a few days before a crucial summit reveals his personal involvement and the emotion that reigned at the time across America. For Ronald Reagan, it was almost a personal matter. It is also a way for him to put pressure on his collaborators.

The president was set to take off for Reykjavík on October 11, and it was only four days before, on the 7, that the objectives to be reached were fixed by his staff. And not a moment too soon. The memorandum drafted by Admiral Poindexter summarized the President's personal goals. The letter was typed and signed by Reagan himself and was addressed to Vice President Bush, Secretary of State George Shultz, Secretary of Defense Caspar Weinberger, CIA Director William Casey, and Director of the United States Information Agency Charles Wick. In this document, the president recalls the reasons for the upcoming summit. "I agreed to meet with Secretary General Gorbachev in Reykjavík in order to accelerate progress in our relations with the Soviet Union. I hope these meetings will be very private and I am preparing to take only a minimal team with me. Following are the goals, expressed one by one:

"—demonstrate my commitment to solving problems in US-Soviet relations, to the degree that the Soviets will desire;

—identify issues for which there is a reasonable prospect of solution, and speed up efforts to resolve them. I will press the Secretary General to agree on acceptable approaches to key issues;

—engage the Soviets in serious and substantive discussions on the whole range of problems in our program. I will not allow the meeting to focus exclusively or disproportionately on arms control, and I will ensure that bilateral issues, regional conflicts and human rights are fully addressed;

—demonstrate to our allies and the American public that the pursuit of our policy toward the Soviet Union, based on realism, strength and dialogue, has created the potential for effective negotiations with the Soviet Union. I will of course continue to avoid preventive and unilateral concessions and will resist Soviet pressure and threats."

It is a true profession of faith that would not entirely stand the test of time.

## In the Mind of Gorbachev

Despite the hasty preparations for the summit, the Americans obviously were doing their best to leave nothing to chance. Above all, the presidential entourage wanted to identify the ulterior motives of the Soviets. Preparing Reagan for the real objectives of Gorbachev and his reaction to American proposals was an urgent priority. Two documents classified at the time as "top secret" but just recently declassified, reveal what the White House really thought of the Soviet leader and how Reagan's counselors prepared the American president for the meetings in Reykjavík.

A document for Ronald Reagan from October 2, recently declassified, dealing with "how to maximize your leverage, what Gorbachev wants," focuses on the goals of the Kremlin. "Its main goals now and in the future: forcing your administration to deflate the foreign and defense policies that challenge the USSR (e.g. SDI and support for anti-Communist rebels) or, failing that, create political pressure inside the U.S. and NATO to make sure your successor will be more accommodating." In short, Reagan's entourage feared Washington's will could begin to weaken.

This is followed by Gorbachev's "objectives in Reykjavík." The document begins, "The minimum goal is to continue the process of dialogue, including summits (but not necessarily to reach agreements) . . . The maximum objective he seeks would be agreement on a few issues including the blocking of SDI to facilitate the reduction of nuclear arsenals. He wants this, but does not expect it immediately" from the Americans, the paper continues.

The next paragraph is even more eloquent. "He (Gorbachev) thinks you, or the rest of Washington, want a summit more than he does. He wants to exploit this. He thinks (from Geneva and your correspondence) that you really want a breakthrough towards a nuclear weapons reduction agreement. He wants you to accept his terms and, more importantly, give up the SDI program. . . . He believes that you are likely to appeal to 'justice' and put yourself in his place. He sees the U.S. government and Congress as disorganized and fragmented, but able to influence you to more towards their positions. He expects this extra pressure from Reykjavík and will separate you from Washington's 'hawks.'"

The classified briefing continues, highlighting the upcoming midterm elections, due to be held just three weeks after the Reykjavík Summit. Gorbachev, the authors of this document posit, wants to exploit electoral pressure, hoping for a major concession from the Americans, because "you do not want to return to Washington from a meeting that would be seen as a failure." An opinion not shared by John Poindexter. The national security advisor believes today, in hindsight, that the midterm, congressional elections did not play any significant role in Reykjavík. "I do not remember that during the preparation of the summit, internal affairs played any important role. After Reykjavík, on our return, though, things were different."

The White House's analysis then deals with the internal situation in Moscow and the power games within the Communist Party itself. "Gorbachev needs to show the Soviet people, the elite of the party, his colleagues and the world that he is a statesman on whom we must rely, that he is reasonable and pragmatic, ready to do business, but capable of defending the vital interests of the Soviet Union and its prestige." The advice given to Reagan is direct: "Know your own strengths; be realistic about your own communication goals; do not apologize for your positions, such as human rights; communicate graciously your willingness to organize informal summits in order to have real negotiations; ask him questions that challenge him, but without provoking him."

A second document, also transmitted to President Reagan on October 2, summarizes Gorbachev's positions on all political and diplomatic issues that would be addressed. In the introduction, it reads: "General Secretary Gorbachev will come to the summit in Iceland from a position of strength on the domestic level, and will have much latitude to negotiate. He wants to reach an agreement on arms control, partly to advance his economic program, but he is not really under political or economic pressure to reach an agreement and will probably prefer to ensure a visit In the United States, rather than making too many compromises in Iceland."

Three-and-a-half pages summarize the political and economic situation in the Soviet Union, in terms of Gorbachev's growing power. The new, young Soviet leader awakened the USSR after many years of hesitation and political transition that followed the long agony of Brezhnev. The document notes that Gorbachev has "added political allies within the Politburo," that he is "now supported" by his once and future rival Yegor Ligachev and "that he feels fully in charge, following his long summer vacation in the Crimea and his official travel plans for the rest of this year." More importantly, Gorbachev has marshalled his supporters within the party, especially on foreign policy. The KGB, too, has strengthened its role since 1985, says the American document, with its chief Viktor Chebrikov appearing to be an ally, and the Red Army hierarchy ready to support economic reforms. In short, Gorbachev is free to do pretty much as he likes. "The letter Gorbachev sent to you indicates that the Politburo gave him a mandate to conduct negotiations even without any promise of success," the briefing document concludes. "But beware, he remains a threat. If Gorbachev does not get a result in Iceland, he is quite likely to postpone the summit in Washington, arguing that more preparation is needed to achieve success and hoping that this delay will put more pressure on the United States."

## From the Soviet Side

At the same time, the Kremlin was making its own preparations for the summit. Around Gorbachev, his team was preparing arguments and counterarguments to deploy in his talks with Reagan. But the organization around the Kremlin leader was significantly different. While the American president was advised directly inside the White House, together with diplomats from the State Department and Pentagon experts, the Kremlin leader had to deal with a host of components of the byzantine collectivist system of the Soviet Union. For while Gorbachev succeeded in building a personal support mechanism around him, more than a year after his coming to power he was still institutionally subject to the approval of a multitude of bodies—the Politburo of the Communist Party, a sort of Areopagus of the nation's leading dignitaries; the party's

Central Committee, a broader ruling collective; not to mention the influence of the army and the KGB.

But several declassified documents dating from the days preceding the Reykjavík Summit suggest that Mikhail Gorbachev was in control of the preparations for the disarmament negotiations at every stage—more so even than Reagan. Reinforced by the backing of the Politburo, Gorbachev went to Reykjavík with a virtual carte blanche to snatch an agreement from the Americans. Vitali Kataev was number two in the Department of Defense Industries of the Communist Party. This engineer by training who was involved in the design of the Yuzhnoye ICBM missile, emerged as one of the leaders in disarmament efforts and was directly involved in the development of negotiating strategies with the Americans. Kataev has retained many documents, which help us understand what was going on behind the scenes in the Kremlin.

According to Kataev's records, Gorbachev's advisors appear to be globally on the same wavelength. There is Anatoli Chernyaev, the main foreign affairs advisor, Marshal Akhromeev, who made himself noticed in Reykjavík by his American counterparts, but also by Georgi Kornienko and Yuli Vorontsov, who were responsible for drawing up the first draft of the agenda.

The main topics to be covered were almost identical to those of the Americans. Nevertheless, there was one big exception. While Reagan's entourage insisted on the importance of discussing human rights and regional conflicts (such as

Afghanistan), the Soviets concentrated almost exclusively on the issue of nuclear disarmament, the American threat of Star Wars, and nuclear tests. At the end of a preparatory meeting of the Politburo, Gorbachev summed up the situation in a few words: "Our main goal now is to prevent a new stage in the arms race. If we do not do this, the danger for us will increase. . . . We will lose, because for us today, we are already at the limit of our capacities." In other words, Reagan, though he may not have been immediately aware of it, was on the verge of accomplishing his goal of spending the Soviet Union into the history books. Reykjavík will prove to be one more nail in the coffin of Communism.

On October 5, just before Gorbachev took off for Iceland, the CPSU Central Committee summarized its recommendations. This internal document was signed by Lev Zaikov, in charge of defense industries; KGB head Viktor Chebrikov; Anatoly Dobrynin, nearing the end of a twenty-four-year career as Soviet ambassador to Washington; Alexander Iakovlev, successor to Mikhail Suslov as the party's chief of ideology and later called the father of glasnost; and Sergei Kovalev. In the document, the signatories ask for final approval from the Central Committee, but list the latest advice for negotiations with Reagan a few days later. "Considering the problems of nuclear disarmament, the initial position of the Soviet Union is that the ultimate outcome of any measure in this area must be the complete elimination of nuclear weapons," the document says at the outset, setting up the centerpiece of the Gorbachev surprise in Reykjavík that would catch Reagan and his entire entourage totally off guard. "While moving in this direction, we must ensure equal security on both sides." Clearly, American intelligence had no sense of the interior thinking of the Kremlin. There follows a succession of thematic paragraphs setting up each Soviet position: strategic offensive weapons, medium-range missile, the problems of ABM and the prohibition of nuclear tests, and finally, verification.

For strategic weapons (intercontinental missiles), the signatories stress the USSR and the United States' previous promise to reduce this arsenal by no less than 50 percent. "Throughout this year, we have been convinced that the world is waiting, not only is it waiting, but it demands that these reductions be implemented."

Intermediate missiles, meanwhile, must be "completely eliminated in Europe," the Soviet leaders continue. "As part of this decision, we are even prepared, and no matter how difficult it is for us, to put aside the nuclear potential of Great Britain and France. With regard to the missiles deployed in Asia, "that can be considered in a separate negotiation." In other words, the top Soviet leadership, one week before the crucial summit with the Americans, feels that it is necessary to go fast and strong—establishing a position more radical than that of the Americans in the same period. Gorbachev is intending to make the necessary compromises to get a big deal at any cost with Reagan.

At this meeting, the issue of how to deal with SDI is also decided. "It is very important to ensure mutual acceptance that development and testing in the field of SDI will be permitted within laboratories and that testing outside of the weapons lab and of arms created to strike from space, targets in space or on the ground, will be prohibited."

Before reaching this clearly established position (a drastic reduction of the nuclear arsenal of long and medium-range missiles, acceptance of the American Star Wars project provided that it is limited to the laboratory), the Central Committee had gradually developed its thinking through a series of evolutionary steps. In undated minutes of one meeting, which preceded the declaration of October 5, 1986, the Soviet leaders—Zaikov, Chebrikov, Sokolov, Dobrynin, and Iakovlev—talk about the strategy underlying the positions they would ultimately set forth formally as Gorbachev's working instructions, but which he had clearly established in advance, winning the frank and direct approval of each of these key individuals. Each considers the context of the atmosphere preceding Reykjavík as most favorable for the arrival at a historic agreement. "The meeting in Reykjavík will be conducted in an atmosphere where the peoples of the world, especially in Europe, turn toward the policies of the Soviet Union. In the United States, people are no longer content to wait, but insist on decisions that should end the arms race and the spiral of a world toward nuclear war," says the text of the final document. Then the Soviet leaders talk about the internal situation of the United States. "Reagan accepted this meeting because of the internal situation in the country. It seems that he can no longer maintain a negative position on nuclear issues and US-Soviet relations. For this reason, it will be difficult for him to leave the summit without a positive result. The international situation as a whole is conducive to a breakthrough in Reykjavík on the main points of disarmament."

The Soviet leaders continue to develop their thinking: "From our point of view, it is essential to take advantage of this context and propose to Reagan in Reykjavík an agreement in principle on the most important issues in the nuclear sphere. Depending on the results of these negotiations, clear and binding guidelines must be given to ministers to work on the texts of treaties and agreements that could be signed at a forthcoming summit in Washington." Clearly, the Soviets did not regard the Icelandic summit as an informal or intermediate discussion. They seem ready to go to the heart of the matter and to prepare the outline of a treaty which would remain to be drafted in detail and signed at a forthcoming summit in the United States.

Even earlier, another document goes further into the technical details of the nuclear arsenals, particularly SDI, and ways to control them. It seems to be a working paper from the Foreign Ministry, written between the American acceptance of a summit (September) and the formal recommendations of the Central Committee to Gorbachev (early October). In a section devoted to nuclear tests, the author summarizes the state of the art in the field of weapons that use laser beams. "According to our sources, the Americans have concluded ten underground nuclear tests in order to create a weapon with a laser beam. . . . Since 1980, there have been five underground nuclear tests conducted in our country to study the possibility of creating laser rays using a nuclear device." The author of this report stresses the consequence of a possible treaty totally banning nuclear tests, since the "development of a new generation of nuclear weapons . . . will be excluded—laser rays, high-intensity electromagnetic radiation, kinetics, etc. Obviously, if such a ban on any nuclear test is to come into force, it must concern all parties. Any unilateral termination by the Soviet Union would result in the military-technical superiority of the United States in the field of nuclear weapons, especially for the development of new-generation strategic ammunition."

The author of this analysis later mentions the intelligence assembled on SDI by the KGB and other Soviet defense agencies and by the Academy of Sciences. But he also insists on the "lack of reliable information about the adversary," that is, the United States. According to his findings, "the full deployment of a missile defense system in space can be ready after 2010." In short, according to the calculations of this expert, a Star Wars system, so dear to Reagan, could not be deployed for another twenty-five years at the earliest. He even answers the crucial question: "The USSR is between four and five years behind in research on a space defense system."

## Defensive or Offensive?

Not only were the Soviets seemingly late, by their own admission, in the pursuit of a Star Wars space weapons system, but they also fear the offensive aspect of SDI. As we have seen, Ronald Reagan referred only to a "defense" system. According to the Soviet analyst, however, "any space system that carries weapons is both offensive and defensive." And he goes further, questioning the sincerity of the Americans. "There is no basis for separating strike systems from space into two, offensive and defensive, categories. This distinction is useful for the United States to hide the real goals of creating SDI. In reality, it is an offensive strategic system designed to destroy the nuclear warheads of our missiles and other objects in space, on Earth and in the air." But in any case, "the United States will not be able to deploy these elements without our realizing it." Mistrust is therefore central to the Soviet point of view.

## Heading to Iceland

A few days before the president's departure for Iceland, Reagan's advisors accelerated the pace of the notes being prepared for the conference. One NSC member reminded the president that "the social functions will be minimal" in order to focus on the discussions. Another worried that "Gorbachev may have a climatic advantage," being more accustomed to the Icelandic cold than Reagan.

Bill Henkel, head of the Reagan advance team, arrived before the president and his delegation. A few days before the departure of Reagan from Washington, he sends a cable signaling the situation in Reykjavík. The US embassy and the hotels are ready to host the delegation. Henkel recalls that the Icelandic government had by decree reserved four hotels for a total of nearly 550 rooms and that the Keflavík air base could accommodate 200 members of the technical staff—far above the delegation's needs, but the security of the president of the United States was considered priceless by the Icelandic government. No tourist would be allowed in any hotel occupied by the delegation. Ronald Reagan would sleep at the resience of the US ambassador with a minimal entourage. "The cooperation [of the Icelandic government] is exceptional," notes Henkel. But he warns there are snow and blizzard conditions. Finally, he adds that "the Soviets had requested ninety-five rooms" and that there is "a rumor of the arrival of a cruise ship" for the Gorbachev delegation.

At the White House, preparations were being refined. The seats on Air Force One, a Boeing 707 put into service under Richard Nixon's presidency in 1973, and a far cry from the spacious 747 in use today, are distributed with caution. With its limited capacity—a private cabin for the president and first lady, a dining room, a lounge for the advisers, then the back of the plane dedicated to the guests, and the least comfortable rows to the press—Air Force One could accommodate fifty-two passengers and a crew of eighteen. Accompanying the president were Shultz, Regan, Poindexter, and a handful of aides. Nancy Reagan would remain in Washington, the Icelandic summit not being an official meeting. This would turn out to be one of the crucial missteps of the entire trip.

The president's travel file included a note on the history of Iceland, which Reagan could draw from for a short arrival speech at the Reykjavík airport and when he met the nation's leaders—President Vigdís Finnbogadóttir, the world's first democratically elected female head of state, Prime Minister Steingrimur Hermannsson, and Foreign Minister Matthias Árni Mathiesen. They would not participate in the meetings between the two powers, but agreed to serve as the hosts.

Just before takeoff, the American media seemed skeptical about the idea of the meeting. In editorials, more or less discreetly expressed, there was the fear of being manipulated by Gorbachev. Tom Brokaw, anchor of the *NBC Nightly News*, said on the air that "the most obvious concern is that Mr. Reagan surrendered to the Soviets, releasing a person accused of espionage and is now meeting (Soviets) on neutral ground, two things he had promised never to do." Dan Rather, on CBS, was even clearer. "In private, some close advisers of Reagan fear that to have accepted the summit in Iceland wanted by the Soviets is a mistake." *The Washington Post*, for its part, merely noted that an "agreement is possible on some issues of nuclear armaments."

But *Newsweek* played the anxiety card: "Danger at the top?" asked the cover story, with a picture of Gorbachev and Reagan shaking hands in Geneva, and the mention of an article by Henry Kissinger, Richard Nixon's savvy secretary of state.

In any case, both the American and Soviet observers and members of the press did not yet fully understand what was hanging in the balance, barely 200 miles from the Arctic Circle, on the lip of an historic moment. Forty-eight hours to change the world.

# SIX

# *Reykjavík, Day 1*

Thursday, October 9, 1986. The time has finally arrived.

9:45 A.M., Andrews Air Force Base, outside Washington. The engines of Air Force One are turning. Ronald Reagan has just stepped off Marine One, the helicopter which has airlifted him from the White House lawn to the foot of the stairway of his 707 jet. As he bounds up the steps, he turns at the door, pausing for a farewell salute before entering his private quarters, at the front of the aircraft. The president knows he is flying to an all but unknown destination and certainly an uncertain rendezvous. The flight plan indicates he will land in

Reykjavík, the capital of Iceland, at 7:05 P.M. local time. But something deep inside him suggests that, in so many ways, this is a trip unlike any he has taken on this same aircraft. He'd responded positively to Mikhail Gorbachev's proposal barely a month before. He knows the agenda, the priority to reach some accord on critical nuclear issues. But how far will the two leaders actually go? What arguments and counterarguments will be made? Will there be any agreement? All this Ronald Reagan does not know. He does want to convince his counterpart of the need for a summit in Washington in the near future. He also realizes that American voters will have their eyes on his every nuance, every gesture, certainly every result.

The advisers and cabinet secretaries who make the trip with him in Air Force One say they are ready for every eventuality. "There was a unique sensation of uncertainty," recalls George Shultz, the secretary of state. The meeting happened so suddenly. Now, nothing seems predictable. The congressional midterm elections are barely three weeks away, and the president was supposed to have been on the road, campaigning for a Republican-controlled Congress that would help him achieve his broad agenda in the last two years of his presidency. Perhaps this summit will be even more valuable than a trip across the American heartland. "The team seems enthusiastic," Shultz recalls. "On our way to Reykjavík, the atmosphere is positive. We want this meeting to be a prelude, a step to set an agenda for the upcoming summit in

Washington. We have taken a full team so we can respond effectively to what might happen."

"Shultz and Weinberger are a little uncomfortable because we've had so little time to prepare," said Admiral John Poindexter, the national security advisor. "But overall, diplomats in the State Department are more optimistic. When we land at the military base outside Reykjavík, my immediate impression is that it looks like the surface of the moon. Very cold. Very flat. An inhospitable environment."

Gorbachev himself has an identical view. With his delegation, he arrives the next day, Friday October 10, in the afternoon. "It was for us an unknown world: no vegetation, nothing but erratic rocks and stones," he would write. "The sky cleared and covered itself in incessant motion, and it rained every half hour." October near the Arctic Circle.

Still, nothing has been left to chance in terms of preparations. Reagan and his team arrive on Thursday night. The first meetings with Gorbachev and his entourage are scheduled for Saturday morning. There is all day Friday to prepare, to establish a final strategy.

The Soviets are dispersed in several places. "I wanted to know more about this unique country," Gorbachev says, "but unfortunately, it was impossible for me to visit anything." Only his wife Raisa has a personalized program. "Reykjavík and Iceland in general are not particularly hospitable in October," smiles Pavel Palazchenko, Gorbachev's interpreter. "They put me in a comfortable hotel, with a pool and gym, but I only stayed one night. Then I had to go with the rest of the delegation to the Soviet embassy."

## Welcome to Höfdi House

The place chosen by the Icelandic government is a vast home, situated on the edge of the ocean. Höfdi House, classified as a historical monument, has had a singular existence. It was built in 1909 on the orders of the consul general of France, Jean-Paul Brillouin, imported from Norway (the diplomat's wife was Norwegian), and assembled in Reykjavík. The house was then sold several times, before it landed in the hands of the British consul in 1938, where Winston Churchill and Marlene Dietrich were received, among others. In 1958, Höfdi (meaning "cap") was bought by the municipality of Reykjavík after the discovery of geothermal springs. Years of decrepitude followed before it was finally restored and today brings together several collections of Icelandic art. Rumor even says the house may be haunted. In short, it was a most appropriate venue for the extraordinary events to come.

Set on the top of a cliff with a view of the North Atlantic, Höfdi is surrounded by a broad lawn. Entirely made of wood, painted white, and covered with a slate roof, the building is built on a quasi-symmetrical plan. The entire structure is not very large, and certainly could not host a formal international conference. But the intimacy of the place has been approved by the White House and the Kremlin. It is perfect for the informal negotiations that are planned, especially since the summit is closed to the press, which will only be allowed to stake out the left side of the house, in front of the circular drive that will welcome the official limousines.

Just eight steps lead to the main door, which leads to the foyer, with a staircase to the second floor. On the ground floor, in the front, is a living room with a window overlooking the ocean. Two armchairs are arranged for the two leaders, allowing photographers to immortalize the scene briefly before being escorted out. On the left is a room with a full-length table for discussions between the full delegations. To the right, a smaller salon reserved for face-to-face discussions.

The second floor is perfectly symmetrical. The left side is reserved for the Americans; the right side, the Soviets. In the center, a large room can be used for meetings between the two teams. On each side are two rooms for advisors in each delegation.

For the Americans, landing just in time for dinner Thursday night, Friday is devoted to the final strategy sessions. "Early in the morning, the president meets with some of his advisors to talk about the program for the day and is briefed on the events of the night," reads the official timeline. At 10 A.M., Secretary of State Shultz and his entourage work at the embassy residence. At eleven o'clock, Donald Regan convenes a group at the Holt

Hotel to review security and organizational issues for the following day. At 11:30, President Reagan attends the first substantive briefing in the dining room of the American embassy with Shultz, Regan, Poindexter, and all the NSC members and diplomatic advisers: press secretary Larry Speakes, Henkel, Thoms, state department negotiator Rozanne Ridgway, Jack Matlock, Paul Nitze, and General Robert Linhard, and after a pause for lunch, Richard Perle of the Pentagon. Between 4:30 and 5:10 P.M., Reagan talks with the president of Iceland. A gesture of politeness and protocol.

Meanwhile, pool reporters who have traveled aboard Air Force One, but who will not be able to attend any meetings, are briefed by Larry Speakes, notably on the subject of nuclear tests. And that evening, the president dines with Secretary Shultz, Regan, Admiral Poindexter, and has the opportunity to make a final review of the most critical issues.

## D-Day

Ten fifteen, Saturday morning.

The American delegation leaves the embassy for Höfdi. Both sides have agreed that Reagan will be the host for the first negotiating session. So he arrives first. A few minutes later, the armored limousine of the general secretary of the Soviet Union arrives slowly, under a steady drizzle, maneuvering across the roundabout in front of the house. The ground is wet and the wind waves the red flag on the car's fender. Gorbachev is dressed in a long black coat. He holds his hat in his hand and, as he walks to the main entrance, gives a perfunctory wave to the journalists at the left of the building before slowly ascending the steps. An attendant opens the door, and Reagan immediately walks through to greet him. The two men shake hands on the steps. The flashes of the cameras sound. The two leaders smile but seem tense. They exchange a few words. Reagan gestures to the wet ground, Gorbachev points his finger at his watch. The journalists are shouting. "The weather!" Reagan replies, adding "Well, here we are," to several indistinct questions. Finally, the two leaders plunge through the entrance.

A few minutes later, the two men are seated in the central lounge, on the ground floor, posing for photographers and television cameras—the only time the press will be able to enter the house. The room is relatively dark, the sun obstructed by heavy gray clouds. The ocean, visible through the large window behind them, seems agitated. A fire crackles in the stone fireplace and the carpet with its dark, Bordeaux patterns add to the country home atmosphere. The two exchange a few words, smile. Gorbachev seems impatient for discussions to begin.

"Höfdi is a very picturesque place," recalls John Poindexter. "This is very comfortable. Once the photographers and cameramen leave the room, both sides find themselves alone. The atmosphere is very special. On the first morning, the meeting is between President Reagan, Gorbachev, Shevardnadze, Shultz and two interpreters. I'm standing in a corner with Marshal Akhromeyev, the Soviet equivalent of our chairman of the Joint Chiefs of Staff. He's rather small, with gray hair. It's funny, because our own joint chief, Jack Vessey, is also a small gray-haired man. They look the same." Poindexter smiles in recollection.

Poindexter turns to Akhromeyev. Quickly, a translator approaches. "I'm sure he understands English, but he speaks to me in Russian," Poindexter continues. "I say to him, 'You look like our General Vessey.' And then he says, 'I am the Last of the Mohicans.' He grabs me and says he is a big fan of James Fenimore Cooper, the author of this classic. Akhromeyev says he is the last in the military hierarchy of the USSR to have fought during the Second World War. Hence this literary reference."

## Discussions Finally Begin

While the two leaders break the ice, the delegations get down to business, specialists on both sides facing off. As Poindexter recalls: "With Akhromeyev, we talked about SDI. I explained we were trying to develop a response to a first attack, and that it would lead to a better environment in time against any other dangerous nations that might develop nuclear weapons. I also said that the president was willing to share this technology [with the Soviets]."

According to Admiral Poindexter, Akhromeyev immediately counterattacked. "He told me that Reagan would not be in office forever, so it was necessary to ensure that any future president had the same intent. 'Ronald Reagan's successor may well be someone more aggressive and unwilling to collaborate,' Akhromeyev said. 'Hence our caution, even mistrust, in terms of implementation.' I think they did not believe us when we said we were willing to share the technology. After this first exchange, I felt very strongly that we would be unable to agree on the reduction of nuclear weapons that we'd hoped for. And I knew the president would not give up the SDI program."

It's now 10:40 A.M. The first tête-à-tête begins, with only the two leaders and their interpreters, accompanied on the American side by a note-taker, Jack Matlock, the Soviet specialist in the NSC and later ambassador to Moscow.

"I am very pleased that you have proposed this meeting, since it is important to ensure that your visit to the United States is as successful as possible," begins Reagan as host.

"We are very grateful to you for having accepted," Gorbachev replies politely.

"What topic would you like to start with?" Reagan asks.

The general secretary proposes to begin with a general exchange of views and then proceed to a more detailed study of the Soviet proposal in the presence of the two foreign ministers. Reagan accepts without hesitation.

"All the themes are important," says the American president. "We are particularly interested in the reduction of strategic weapons and we have agreed in Geneva at the level of fifty percent. The world is looking at us, hoping we can get there." The leader of the "free world" insists "on the pressure of public opinion that wants cooperation between the two powers." And Reagan is solemn. "I am convinced that our situation is unique. We are here, the two of us, sitting together in the same room, and maybe we will solve the problem of whether there will be peace or war in the world. We both want peace, the goal is to strengthen confidence and reduce the mutual suspicion between our two peoples."

## Gorbachev's Poker Move

After a few minutes of pleasantries, Gorbachev launches into his argument: "The Geneva Summit created a mechanism of movement in our relations. There have been blows and even some black eyes in the wake of Geneva. But the central issue is to prevent a nuclear threat. We have worked a lot in Geneva, but matters are virtually deadlocked. We have to focus on one or two options."

"We have already agreed on a 50 percent reduction in strategic weapons," Reagan interjects. "Apparently, that's more than what you are willing to accept. We have proposed a limit of 4,500 nuclear warheads and you countered with a number of 6,400 to

6,800. That is too much, in our view, because it still threatens the destruction of the entire planet." Reagan then mentions a possible "interim agreement" with an intermediate number of 5,500 authorized nuclear warheads.

The Soviet leader replies that he will go into details later, but he wishes to continue his introduction. "The leadership of the USSR wants to solve the problem of the nuclear arms race," he says. In working towards the elimination of nuclear weapons, there must be parity and equality at every stage. Nothing else is acceptable.

Reagan agrees, but then insists on the question of verification. "It reminds me of the old Russian proverb 'doveryai no proveryai': 'trust but verify.'"

Gorbachev smiles. "I know this proverb well! Yes, I agree with you on inspections," he says, but then points to the pressures around them. "We cannot afford to fail. It would be a scandal if we continued to see each other without reaching an agreement."

"Yes, but to agree on the number of nuclear warheads will not be enough," replies Reagan. Let us not forget that this will only be an intermediate step towards the complete elimination of nuclear weapons."

It is now 11:30 A.M. The two men have finished their opening remarks and decide to invite in Secretary of State George Shultz and Foreign Minister Eduard Shevardnadze. It's time to get to the heart of the matter. Gorbachev raises some concrete proposals. He enumerates them, referring to notes, point by point, without being interrupted by the Americans.

In the area of strategic nuclear weapons, that is, intercontinental ballistic missiles, he says the Soviets want a 50 percent reduction, no less. "Initially, we were in favor of a 50 percent reduction for all missiles that can reach our respective territories. But now we are prepared to leave out the intermediate range missiles, which can be negotiated separately. This is a major concession on our part," he observes.

Gorbachev begins to lay out his proposal in detail. As he proceeds, it becomes increasingly clear that this is the very reason for his desire to meet in Reykjavík. "I would like to proclaim precisely, firmly and clearly that we are in favor of a solution to the problem which will lead in the end, to the complete liquidation of nuclear weapons, which would ensure equality and equal security for the United States and the Soviet Union at all stages along the way toward this goal. Any other approach would be unintelligible, unrealistic and unacceptable. We hope that the United States would act in the same way."

To which Reagan replies: "We have exactly the same feelings."

The path toward a world of zero nukes is suddenly open on the table.

Gorbachev reviews the trajectory of negotiations that have occupied the months between Geneva and Reykjavík, then returns to his startling new proposal. It is certainly audacious and takes the American camp by surprise. "I will now present our proposals on strategic offensive weapons," Gorbachev says. "Both we Soviets and the US have worked in the past toward fifty percent reduction proposals. We also talked about this in Geneva. However, since then, several variables have been discussed at the negotiating table. I would now like to confirm that the Soviet leadership wants a specific reduction of strategic offensive weapons by fifty percent. No less."

A moment passes. This was no real surprise. Then Mikhail Gorbachev solemnly declares: "This, Mr. President, is our package of proposals on all aspects of nuclear weapons reduction. I suggest that you and I here in Reykjavík give instructions to the appropriate departments—the Ministries of Foreign Affairs and others—to jointly develop these agreements that we will sign during my visit to Washington."

In the course of presenting this package, Gorbachev does not forget intermediate-range missiles—one of the key points on which the two men have not agreed immediately. "We propose a total elimination of these missiles in Europe and we are going to make a major concession: we agree not to count the British and French nuclear forces. It is not nothing, because they are forces far from negligible in number and in quality. So it's an important compromise," he observes. The Soviet leader continues by addressing a crucial point for the Americans: the Asian-based intermediate missiles. "In a spirit of compromise, the United States should withdraw this issue from negotiations," Gorbachev suggests. "Or at least agree to continue negotiations separately, while those from Europe are eliminated. We could freeze missiles with a range of less than 625 miles."

Now comes the ABM Treaty. The situation may seem complex. This text, signed at the same time as the SALT agreements in 1972, "prohibits deploying a system to defend the national territory against a strategic ballistic missile attack." In short, these are defensive weapons, in contrast to so-called "offensive" missiles. At the time, when Nixon and Brezhnev signed a nuclear arms limitation (not reduction) treaty, they wanted to ban any defensive system in the event of an attack. The logic was simple—the more sophisticated the defense, the more likely is a massive attack. Moreover, this treaty was required to be reviewed every five years by the two signatories. And since 1974, an amendment has been added to the main text. It allows an exception: the creation of a missile deployment zone (ABM) around the capital of the country or around an intercontinental missile launch base. The Soviets chose Moscow; the Americans, their North Dakota missile base.

In Reykjavík, Gorbachev now insists on finding a period when the two sides would not withdraw from the ABM Treaty. "We are proposing a compromise by which we adopt the US approach not to withdraw and to open a period of negotiations thereafter," says the Soviet leader. In this period, Gorbachev wants the two nations to make a firm commitment to abide by the ABM Treaty. And therefore not to create a new defense system, for example, the SDI.

"What is important here is to understand each other," Gorbachev says. "This will allow us to research and test in the laboratory, but not outside laboratories, including space weapons that can strike objects in space and on land." Specifically, Gorbachev is proposing a period of "ten years, no less" when neither side can leave the ABM Treaty, coupled with a period of negotiations between three and five years on missile defense. In other words, pushing off even the first deployed test of an SDI system for at least a decade.

Gorbachev is finally ready to give the floor to his counterpart. Having played his ace card, to reassure him of his good intentions, he confirms "the Soviet Union is ready to carry out all necessary verifications by all appropriate means, though of course we expect you to do the same." He then hands Reagan a file recapitulating in English all the Soviet positions he has just laid out.

## Reagan Point Blank

Now, it's Ronald Reagan's turn. He begins by thanking his counterpart. "It's encouraging," he says. But some differences remain. Reagan agrees on the zero-missile option for Europe, but there must be a reduction of such missiles in Asia. They are mobile and can very well be repositioned to target Europe on short notice. Reagan then switches to intercontinental missiles. "We would also like to go to zero, but we are drawing a line on the proposals you have made on the ABM Treaty. Our argument is that SDI will make possible the elimination of nuclear weapons. So we could propose a treaty that would cover the

ABM treaty and allow both sides to conduct nuclear tests in the presence of representatives from the other side." Reagan stresses that this new treaty will also be imposed, of course, on their successors.

Gorbachev appears vexed by Reagan's reaction. "I hope these are only preliminary remarks," he replies to the American president. "We have made new proposals that have never been discussed before. You must study them carefully. On the ABM Treaty, we do not understand. We have proposed preserving it and strengthening it and you want to destroy it."

Somewhat recovering, the general secretary politely lobs the ball back to his opponent's side. "I hope you will study our new proposals carefully. We would really appreciate your giving us a point-by-point answer. It is important for us, and for the United States, to know what you can accept and what you cannot accept, and why."

"We'll look at your proposals," Reagan replies. "But you refuse to see one thing: if SDI research is successful, we can eliminate nuclear weapons."

Gorbachev, irritated, sums up, recalling that this had already been the subject of negotiations at their previous meeting in Geneva. "But of course, I'm ready to talk about it again if you wish."

It's half past noon. Time for lunch.

At that point, the teams split. The leaders leave Höfdi for their respective residences, accompanied by their closest advisors.

The others remain on-site to continue the work, group by group, each on a single, thematic file. Lunch lasts an hour. At 2 P.M., the expert groups link up with the leaders at their leaders' residences. But the ball is now in the camp of the Americans, to respond to the precise proposals made by the Soviets. Reagan "decides to propose a series of two working sessions, one on human rights and the other on the control of nuclear weapons," according to an internal White House memorandum. The two leaders return to Höfdi at three fifteen. The Soviet team appears serene and patient. After all, it is now the turn of the Americans to reply point by point to the proposals the Soviets made in the morning. On the American side, Colonel Robert E. Linhard, in charge of disarmament issues, and Jack Matlock, the specialist on Soviet issues, stay upstairs to prepare for the subsequent sessions in detail.

As soon as Reagan and Gorbachev are installed in their armchairs, and as the outside light begins to fade through the bay window in the middle of the afternoon, the American president takes the floor and holds it for some time. He begins by confirming his intention to aim for a "50 percent reduction," but points to a disagreement on the number of nuclear warheads to be abolished, since the vast bulk of these missiles already have the capacity to carry a number of independently targeted warheads. Reagan then proposes a limit on "air-to-ground cruise missiles," launched from aircraft, "but no limitation on other airborne bomber armaments. Regarding your proposal on intermediate missiles, I am disappointed," Reagan continues. While he is satisfied with the abolition of missiles in Europe, he calls for a "proportional reduction in Asia," observing that they remain dangerous, mobile, and capable of targeting European allies of the Americans.

## The SDI Spine

Finally, President Reagan turns to what seems to be increasingly the principal stumbling block: "Star Wars."

"You are worried that this defense system will be used to attack," he says, calling out Gorbachev directly on what is clearly the principal fear of the Soviet leader. "I can assure you that this is not the SDI principle. Yes, I've heard concerns about the possibility of destroying ground targets from weapons in space. But there are no weapons that are more reliable, more efficient and faster than ballistic missiles. We already have an agreement that prohibits the deployment of weapons of mass destruction in outer space. [. . .] We do not have the ability to carry out a first strike and I can assure you that's not our goal." In a valiant effort to win the support of his opponent, the American guarantees that he is ready to "share any of our advances in strategic defense" with the USSR.

After this presentation, Gorbachev feels a need to clarify matters. In his inimitable laser-like style, he returns to the offensive, hoping to deal a knockout blow to an argument from an opponent. "Before I respond, Mr. President, at least briefly to the many questions you have raised, I would like to ask you a few questions for clarification. If I understand correctly, you share our goal of reducing strategic offensive missiles by 50 percent?" Reagan answers with a simple "Yes."

"At the same time," continues the Soviet leader, "as I understand it, the figures you have quoted correspond to those discussed in Geneva, namely a reduction of 30 percent."

Reagan responds: "We offered 6,000 units."

Immediately, George Shultz intervenes to the rescue of his president. "This level would include 4,500 nuclear warheads on ballistic missiles and fifteen hundred missiles launched by air."

The Soviet leader seems to chew this over for a moment, then continues his explanation by taking on Shultz directly. "A lot of things have already been said about these options and you know that this has led to a stalemate," he shoots back coldly. "What I am proposing is this: we agree that strategic weapons are reduced by 50 percent. And this includes a reduction in all types of armaments in our offensive arsenal by half: missiles launched from the ground, submarines, and bombers. As a result, the entire range of offensive weapons will be reduced by half . . . This is a simple, proportional solution that everyone will understand."

Suddenly, Ronald Reagan seems on the defensive. Gorbachev seizes the opportunity to go for checkmate, as if he felt he were taking the lead in a chess game. Finally, the president, seeking to buy time, dismisses the Soviet leader's proposals with an offhanded, "This is something that can be discussed, if you accept the expert meetings that we propose. I cannot say anything definitive for now, I do not know all the figures. But it seems to me that you will keep some advantage with a 50 percent reduction, since after all you have more of everything and so you will still have more with a cut in half." The American hesitates, but what he has just advanced is true. Conventional and even nuclear forces are more numerous on the Soviet side. Reagan even points out that in the US bomber fleet (precisely 518 aircraft, he says), "Many are old and no longer part of our [operational] force."

At that moment, Secretary of State Shultz cuts in with an observation that will transform the entire conversation: "Well, even if it is a reduction by half, this proposal seems to me to be interesting, even audacious." In one sentence, the head of US diplomacy emphasizes the prevarication of his own president and takes a clear position in favor of the Soviet proposal. Gorbachev feels the winds shifting dramatically. A consummate politician, he snatches the clear advantage that's just been handed to him. "Does that mean you're interested?" he asks.

Reagan seeks desperately to reclaim the advantage. "So do you agree to organize a meeting tonight with the experts?"

"We will talk about it," Gorbachev concedes.

It is getting late in Reykjavík. The time spent parsing the number of missiles and nuclear warheads has caused the official agenda to fall somewhat behind schedule. Fatigue and tension are felt equally on both sides of the table. In the room, the six people present (Reagan, Shultz, Gorbachev, Shevardnadze, and the two interpreters) are not very comfortable, straddling relatively spartan chairs, except for the two heavy easy chairs for the two heads of state.

The conversation slides into the issue of intermediate missiles, the Pershing II and the SS-20 installed in Europe and the SS-18 in Asia. Gorbachev returns to his most important concession—the nuclear arsenal of the United Kingdom and France will not be counted in the totality of reductions. In other words, the United States will always be able to count on the strength of its two most loyal allies, who will not be subject to any cutbacks. Again, Gorbachev is most direct, to the point of interrupting Shultz coldly: "I want to hear the president's opinion. Understood? Not yours."

"All this seems simple to me," the general secretary summarizes. "You brought your missiles to Europe and you do not want to withdraw. If that's it, say so! As for our missiles in Asia, they will not reach Europe. [. . .] But what I would like to ask you, Mr. President, is this: if a solution is found for Asia, would you agree to a zero option in Europe?"

Reagan replies monosyllabically, "Yes."

The two leaders then return to the ABM Treaty and the proposal to respect it for at least the next ten years. This provides Gorbachev the opportunity to extrapolate, "Therefore, the logic is that we reinforce the ABM Treaty and at the same time you confine SDI to the laboratory." After all, in the end, SDI is little more than a sophisticated ABM. A little later, he articulates for the first time his fears about Star Wars. "If your laboratory research motivates you to create such a system and considering that America has a lot of money, our response will necessarily be different, that is to say asymmetric." Parsing this reaction allows us to understand the fundamental fear of a Soviet Union, which, from a purely financial perspective, is utterly incapable of engaging in a race for the arming of space. Which may be precisely what Ronald Reagan had in mind from the beginning.

Meanwhile, it's time to wind up this second session. But first, Reagan wants to return to SDI. "A few words in conclusion," he says. "You say you do not need SDI, but you might very well have your own parallel program, and if you see that you have something a little better, then perhaps you might share it with us."

Gorbachev cuts in immediately: "Excuse me, Mr. President, but I do not take your idea of sharing SDI seriously. You don't want to share your know-how in oil exploration, machine tools or even dairy equipment, and you'd be willing to share SDI, which you are treating as if it were a second American Revolution? Revolutions don't happen often. It would be better to be realistic and pragmatic."

Reagan, by now a little upset, replies that "If I didn't think SDI could be shared, I would have rejected it myself."

## Human Rights in the USSR . . . and the United States

Before leaving, Reagan insists on talking about issues other than disarmament, and in particular human rights. Gorbachev notes with astonishment that the American president had prepared a file for him. He takes it in his hands while listening intently. Reagan begins to speak—first, touching on the emigration of the Jews of Russia, spouses and families separated by the Iron Curtain, citizens with dual citizenship. The folder includes lists of names, charts, tables. Gorbachev nods his head. And then lashes out: "We too are worried about human rights in the United States."

The two men separate at 5:45 P.M., each returning to their quarters for dinner. The American advisers—Shultz, Poindexter, Regan, plus five other counselors—join their president for a detailed debriefing of the first day. For thirty minutes, the American team reviews the points raised with the Soviets. The two leaders had agreed that their two groups of experts would meet that night after eight o'clock in Höfdi to discuss and draw up proposals to be dealt with by the two foreign ministers. "The president was in a light mood," recalls Poindexter. "He was a man sure of himself and of his convictions."

After the dinner of the small committee, the groups of experts meet in Höfdi to move forward as much as possible on all subjects. As the White House report of the discussion notes, "Marshal Akhromeyev was ready for a frank discussion and willing to explore every question as seen from both sides."

## Poindexter's Secret Initiative

That evening, in the American camp, there's no camouflaging their stupefaction. "Yes, we were surprised" by the proposals put forward by Gorbachev and his concessions, John Poindexter reveals years later. "But at the end of that first day, I realized we were going to run into a bigger problem. I could see what was going on. Gorbachev spread all these concessions on the table, but he was asking us to abandon SDI. The problem for the American camp was that it would mean we would leave without an agreement. And from a public relations point of view, that would not have been good. So it was I who summarized at the dinner of the four principals of our delegation [Shultz, Regan, Poindexter, and the President], the situation as I saw it. And nobody disagreed with my position. It was then that I decided to bring up the proposal of [Casper] Weinberger, the secretary of defense, who did not come to Reykjavík. He had given it to me, but it had not yet been circulated among us. I said that if we did not make the kind of strong move that Weinberger was suggesting, if we had nothing to propose to counter the Soviet proposal, we would find ourselves in great difficulty. The president agreed. Shultz too. And we asked our experts to consider it that night. Richard Perle, who represented Cap, was not surprised. He must have known. But the guys in the state department were surprised."

What is this secret initiative prepared by Weinberger and guarded so jealously by Poindexter? "In his note, the secretary of defense made a totally new proposal," explains the former national security advisor. "He proposed to get rid of all ground-based missile bases. In short, nuclear missiles would only be launched from bombers or submarines—mobile, stealth or hidden launchers. For the secretary of defense, this represented an advantage by reducing the number of targets for the Soviets on American soil, while providing a positive proposal in the negotiations. I found this plan very interesting and I kept it in my pocket. None of our teams were working on such a bold proposal. I had told Cap that I would reveal this joker to the president at the best possible moment."

Weinberger was persuaded that the Soviets "would never accept it," Poindexter confesses. "It was just too big a change. From our point of view, in the United States, we always considered land bases to be more problematic than submarines, because they were easy targets." In 1982 and 1983, the White House tried to push for the construction of new land bases, according to Poindexter. "But Congress refused, not wanting to spend millions in offensive weapons. This is how the idea of SDI was born as a defensive system."

After dinner, the Americans set up working groups, with instructions to work on this new proposal. Objective: to identify the missile bases to eliminate. In the early morning hours of Day Two, the president will approve the new document that will be proposed at that morning's meeting with Mikhail Gorbachev.

◆

For George Shultz, the record of the first day is positive: "We made no concessions, but the Soviets moved much further than anyone could have thought. President Reagan had kept his ground, defending its positions effectively. The two men were in agreement on the elimination of nuclear weapons, and significant progress seemed possible, according to Reagan's own words." But that evening, the very nature of the summit changed. "The working groups system meant that a US-Soviet negotiation had been launched," the chief US diplomat recalls.

During the night, the American negotiators are struggling. Paul Nitze in particular, accompanied by five other members of the delegation, knock at Shultz's hotel door. It is two o'clock in the morning and he is in a dressing gown. "Nitze saw a chance for real progress, but [arms negotiator, General (ret.) Edward Rowny in our delegation was against the idea of showing any flexibility on our part," Shultz would recall in his memoirs.

Sitting in the small living room of Shultz's hotel suite, they review the number of nuclear warheads. They then agree to limit this level first to 6,000 units, placed on 1,600 "vectors," defined as submarines and planes. According to Richard Perle, "Akhromeyev is ready to agree." The idea is to help the Soviets accept a total equality of arms, and not just a blanket halving of the nuclear arsenal, which would continue to give them an advantage in numbers. The team leaves for Höfdi, where the

Americans are expecting to meet their Soviet counterparts at three o'clock in the morning. "I went back to bed, asking myself how to behave the next day to manage the inevitable pressure—and potential," Shultz would later write.

On the Soviet side, hope is widespread during the night. Gorbachev had made concessions and concrete proposals on the 50 percent cutback in nuclear arsenals. The American reaction remains to be seen the next morning. "Gorbachev assembled the entire delegation and asked me to read my notes," recalls Pavel Palazchenko, interpreter and notetaker. "This lasted at least thirty minutes. Then, for a good quarter of an hour, he spoke to everybody. The atmosphere was rather casual. Everyone was able to express his opinion. I think we all thought we had a chance. We understood that our positions, the mandate given to us by the Politburo, was attractive to the Americans."

That evening, the Soviet camp seems reasonably optimistic. The general secretary gives final instructions for the night's work to his negotiators. "Gorbachev did not like to go into details," Palazchenko says. He asks Akhromeyev to direct these negotiations. "'Do not go too far into limits and sub-limits. Reduce all the figures by half!'" Palazchenko recalls Gorbachev saying. "He ordered discussion of intermediate-range missiles. Of course, when they resumed the conversation with the Americans, it was more complicated than that. But they made a lot of progress during the night. The idea was really to get the negotiations going."

The Soviet camp seems to be united, more so than the Americans in any case. "Absolutely," Palazchenko confirms. This is before problems and doubts emerged within the Soviet army and diplomatic circles in 1988 and 1989. But in October 1986, everyone was on board, united. The instructions given by the Politburo to Gorbachev were rather flexible. At the same time, they included important advances that could be considered concessions. "These concessions had been approved unanimously," Palazchenko recalls. "I knew. Shevardnadze confirmed it to me *a posteriori*. No one disputed the idea of halving the number of SS-18s. This was approved by the Politburo, first by the group of five experts, then by the main group of five."

As the minutes of conversations in the Politburo demonstrate, "these directives contained a certain flexibility and left Gorbachev with the possibility of keeping the proposals in a single package or unbundling them," Palazchenko says. In the latter case, "it would have come down to saying, 'we do not agree on the ABM treaty, on missiles, so we defeat the package.' That was his own responsibility and he assumed it."

The Soviet delegation, even when reduced in size compared with Geneva or other international summits, proves to be larger than anticipated. But, according to Palazchenko, it is effective: "The delegation worked as a unified group. Karpov and Akhromeyev are the most important links." Paul Nitze, who is leading the talks on space, dines for an hour with his Soviet counterpart, drinking vodka along with Palazchenko, translates for the two men.

But very quickly, everyone finds the quarters too cramped in Höfdi. "It was a problem," says Palazchenko. "Some important points were written by Akhromeyev on the steps of the inner staircase, literally. Initially, Gorbachev wanted this summit to be limited and informal. I do not know how it happened, but we found ourselves with more people than expected, and it was not very comfortable."

Still, "after the first day of discussions and the night-long sessions of the experts, the state of mind was positive," concludes Anatoly Chernyaev, the diplomatic adviser to the general secretary. "But it was the next day when everything collapsed."

# SEVEN

# *Reykjavík, Day 2*

The sunrise over Reykjavík is anything but scintillating. On October 12 at this latitude, the sun only emerges for ten hours a day. The sky is already overcast with low-hanging clouds. The temperature hovers between 35 and 43 degrees (Fahrenheit) during the day and the surface of the ocean is disturbed by hardly a ripple. Still, the weather is the last thing Reagan and Gorbachev are considering when they awaken that morning. They have more important issues to worry about. They know their teams have been talking through the night on the second floor of Höfdi House. Two groups have been assembled, as planned: one focusing exclusively on nuclear arms, led by Bob Linhard on the American side and by Marshal Akhromeyev for the Soviets; and another group dealing with other issues such as human rights, bilateral relations, and regional conflicts.

The first meeting between the two leaders starts at 10 A.M. and lasts three-and-a-half hours. Although the two men parted company the previous evening feeling frustrated, they resume their discussion as if nothing is wrong. "This is our third conversation, Mr. President," begins Mikhail Gorbachev. Secretary of State George Shultz and Minister of Foreign Affairs Eduard Shevardnadze are also present. And as always, the four men are accompanied by their interpreters.

The US president is the first to speak, saying he is "disappointed" with the results of the first group's overnight negotiations. He points out, however, that "the two sides have shown a desire to compromise" and "agree on implementing a 50% reduction of strategic offensive arsenals." At last, the Americans have moved their position for the first time. They agree to an overall reduction in the number of strategic ballistic missiles, rather than individual warheads. But regarding intermediate-range missiles, "we have not succeeded in resolving the issue of reducing those missiles in Asia," says Reagan, still summarizing the overnight discussions. "Even though they were discussed at great length." The president explains again that he cannot "ignore the existence of this issue and make progress on an overall agreement."

"These SS-18s (in Asia) are mobile and can easily be moved around. Their presence impacts our Asian allies, as well as our allies in Europe," he says, alluding to South Korea and Japan, then to Western Europe.

But after blowing cold, Reagan shifts and begins blowing hot. "We are willing to accept the number of one hundred nuclear warheads for the USSR and the United States in Europe, if we can agree on the reduction of Soviet missiles in Asia to a level proportional to the deployment of missiles on US territory," he declares.

Mikhail Gorbachev is surprised. "I'd like to sum up the American proposal in precise terms," he says.

He proceeds to repeat the substance of Reagan's offer. "Yes, that's right," the president responds. The two men review their teams' conclusions point by point. Now it's Gorbachev's turn to speak. The general secretary reiterates his determination to reach a concrete agreement with his American counterpart. "We think that the proposals we have brought to Reykjavík are formulated with a substantial constructive element, and not on a philosophical but on a very concrete level. We have made major concessions to the United States in the hope of moving ahead with the arms control talks and working seriously on reducing nuclear weapons. It is my impression that the American side is not taking our position into account or at least, as can be seen, is carrying on the discussion in the same way as in Geneva," one year earlier.

The Soviet leader repeats the same arguments, insisting that his main concession of not including the French and British nuclear arsenals in the total count is significant. Then he turns and suddenly accuses the United States, point blank, of not cooperating: "You and your people think that we have a greater interest in nuclear disarmament than the United States does, and that if you put a little pressure on the Soviet Union it will raise its hands and surrender. This is a dangerous mistake. It is not going to happen. You talk of some kind of intermediate agreement, with which we do not agree. We will not accept palliatives. We want a solution to the problem."

## British and French Forces

Ronald Reagan remains mute, preferring to let his counterpart express his thoughts as Gorbachev turns again to the question of intermediate-range missiles in Europe and Asia.

Finally the American president speaks, but only succeeds in further annoying Gorbachev. "We do not consider the French and British forces as part of NATO," Reagan says, much to the surprise of Gorbachev and Shevardnadze. "Those (nuclear) forces exist for the defense of those countries, their governments have stated that clearly. It appears that they will not be activated in the case, for instance, of an attack on West Germany."

Gorbachev doesn't remain speechless for long. Not missing a beat, he launches into an examination of his own interests in

Europe. "Mr. President, you say that the British and French missiles are not defending West Germany. Well who will defend the GDR [German Democratic Republic]? Czechoslovakia, Romania, and Bulgaria? Who will defend them? That argument does not work. That is the first thing. Second, I remember my talk with Mrs. Thatcher on the question of the British forces, when she tried to convince me of the same thing, that these forces are independent of NATO. I cited her letter sent to the head of the Joint Chiefs of Staff where it says that she appreciates the work done by the American side to re-equip and modernize the British forces. The British do not hide the fact that these forces are integrated into NATO. It is well known in the USSR. And it is known to you. We are not at a press conference, but rather in conversation in a small group, Mr. President. We should not engage in banalities. We know everything about the participation of England and France in NATO and we know which targets these weapons are aimed at, and by whom. I say this to you so frankly because we are talking about exceptionally serious and important matters." Gorbachev is not afraid of revealing this information, clearly given to him by his secret services.

His retort has an unexpected consequence. Rather than feeling antagonized, Reagan reasserts his willingness to reach an overall agreement on nuclear disarmament. Gorbachev then divulges his position within the USSR and even inside the Politburo. Simply put, he knows it is relatively fragile. Or temporary, at any rate. "A year ago, the Soviet Union could not have offered such compromises, and certainly not 2 or 3 years ago," he says. "What will happen if we do not make use of this opportunity? Reykjavík will just be mentioned in passing, nothing more. A shame that all that was missed."

Reagan agrees. "I am in the same position," he responds. "It is possible that before long I will not have the same powers. Why not use the time that we have to make a contribution to the creation of a world free of the nuclear threat?"

The moment takes an even more profound turn when Gorbachev allows his feelings to emerge. "I believe that now, when I sit opposite you, the President of the United States, I can look you in the eye with a clear conscience. We have brought far-reaching proposals. I ask you to appreciate this. One thing is needed to reach agreement, a desire on your side."

Reagan is unmoved and shoots back, "We have gotten a little carried away," then, continuing in a more conciliatory tone, adds, "You said that you are ready to reduce missiles in Asia too. I am glad to hear that."

## Recap

At this point in the conversation Mikhail Gorbachev wants a progress report. He summarizes what the two leaders have approved thus far. "This is our position: elimination of all Soviet and American intermediate-range missiles in Europe, setting aside British and French forces . . . a start to negotiations on missiles in Asia. I will go even further. You put forward the formula of one hundred warheads on Soviet missiles in the Asian part of the USSR and one hundred warheads on U.S. missiles in America. For us this means a several-fold reduction of our missiles. But okay, if the United States is unable to offer us anything else, we agree even with that measure. Even though we see what the situation is in Asia, what is happening in Japan and your own presence in the Pacific. But we are taking this final step to show that we are serious. In this case, would you be ready for a zero level in Europe?" he asks finally.

"We agree with that," replies Reagan.

"Good. I have been waiting for you to start making some concessions," Gorbachev smiles.

So, the question of intermediate-range missiles in Europe and Asia has been resolved. It is the first real agreement achieved in Reykjavík. But naturally the two leaders must now address the main issue: SDI and the ABM Treaty banning all antiballistic missile defense systems. At this stage of the summit it is the major sticking point between the Americans and Soviets.

From the beginning, Gorbachev has been eager for the Americans to abandon the Strategic Defense Initiative. He knows it won't be easy. But halfway through the morning on the last day of negotiations, he is pressed for time. So he loosens up, proposing several very direct arguments. And the atmosphere begins to shift.

"We propose to commit ourselves not to use the right to withdraw from the ABM Treaty for ten years, and during this time to strengthen the treaty. . . . We have also decided to agree that laboratory testing in the SDI area will not be prohibited. In other words, we do not touch the SDI program within the framework of laboratory experiments."

Now the word has been uttered: laboratory. Indeed, what preparations would be involved for a space and military program that could launch into orbit devices capable of generating weaponized laser beams able to bring down a missile in flight? Wouldn't there be a long phase of laboratory testing? Or would it require full-scale implementation or deployment to answer scientists' questions? In any case, Gorbachev decides to lay all his cards on the table at this stage of the encounter between the leaders of the two superpowers, revealing information from Soviet intelligence services.

"We know what phase of development you are in," he says, addressing Reagan and Shultz. "And we know that you have had some breakthroughs in two or three areas. We know, and we ourselves are doing a few things. So, the laboratory phase should not constrain you."

Ronald Reagan doesn't respond for a few seconds. Outside, rain beats down on Höfdi House. It's late morning but the low-hanging clouds are obscuring the weak Arctic sun. Then the President speaks. "The United States never violated the ABM treaty. . . . As for SDI, when we put forward a program of strategic defense we are pursuing the objective of preserving the peace and achieving disarmament. . . . Understand me, I cannot retreat from my positions, renounce what I promised our people. I am serious about sharing this technology with the Soviet Union. Why can't we make this part of the ABM Treaty?"

Then George Shultz steps in. The secretary of state wants to clarify the Soviet argument. "I would like to ask a question," he says. "When you, Mr. General Secretary, speak of complete elimination of nuclear weapons, as far as I understand you are tying this to a ten-year period of non-exercise of the right to withdraw from the ABM Treaty. In other words, do you think this ten-year period will be enough for complete elimination of nuclear weapons? If you have in mind such a connection, this timetable even exceeds your plan for strategic arms and intermediate-range forces. Do you believe that after ten years not a single ballistic missile should be left?"

In his response, Gorbachev confirms the two five-year phases. But he conditions the complete elimination of nuclear arsenals on "respecting the ABM Treaty," observing that "in agreeing to SDI research in a laboratory setting, we are going halfway to meet the President, who is bound by a promise to his people and before the world. We are giving him this opportunity to show that his idea is alive, that we are not burying it, that the United States can continue laboratory work on SDI, but cannot go beyond the framework of research."

At that precise moment the Soviet side seems to be scoring points. A few minutes earlier it had secured an agreement on intermediate-range missiles. And the proposal to allow Star Wars at the laboratory level seems to be a real concession. Looking Ronald Reagan in the eye, Gorbachev has clearly stated that he's giving him a way out. SDI remains alive, but cannot be launched in space for another ten years.

## A "Male Tango"

Paradoxically, this situation seems to make the American president uncomfortable. "Dammit, what kind of agreement are you defending?" he asks, irritated. "I do not understand the charm of the ABM Treaty, which in fact signifies guaranteed mutual destruction," he snaps.

Gorbachev finds it hard to believe. He goes on the offensive again, rather aggressively. "What have we heard from you?" he asks, insinuating that the Americans have made no important concessions. "It is important for you to determine that the true interests of the American side lie in finding mutually acceptable solutions to the problems. We said that President Reagan is a man who does not like to make concessions. I am now convinced of this. But as the American saying goes, 'it takes two to tango' . . . therefore I invite you to a male tango, Mr. President."

But the situation still doesn't improve. During the minutes that follow, the two leaders continue to pass the buck and blame each other for past maneuvering and failures. Ronald Reagan launches into a long tirade on the differences between the two political systems: a democracy and an authoritarian regime. "I understand that you do not trust us, just as we do not trust you. But I am convinced that historical facts are on our side. Long ago Karl Marx said . . ."

Gorbachev can hardly contain himself: "Well, earlier the President referred to Lenin, and now he's moved on to Marx," he quips. "I was very surprised when I heard that just before our meeting in Reykjavík you said in a speech that you remained loyal to the principles set forth by you in your message at Westminster," says the Soviet. "In that speech you said that the Soviet Union is the Evil Empire and called for a crusade against Socialism. . . . What does it mean politically, to make war against us?"

Reagan replies quickly: "The difference between us has always been that we in the United States have a Communist Party whose representatives can vote in elections and even hold elected offices and propagate their philosophy, while you do not have anything like that." The American president pursues his argument, denouncing the USSR's undemocratic single-party system.

Gorbachev shoots back: "Mr. President, if you want to carry out such a broad debate on political, ideological and ethical issues, I am ready for it. But wouldn't it be better to stop this argument and return to the issues that we have not resolved?"

"Yes, I think so," Reagan says.

But Gorbachev plows ahead. "I do not want to argue with you and I respect your independent nature, and your views and ideas. And I am convinced that if you and I have different ideological ideas, that is not a reason to shoot at each other. On the contrary, I am convinced that in addition to political relations, purely human relations are also possible between us."

Reagan likes this and responds with one of his inimitable jokes: "Unquestionably. And I would even like to try to convince you to join the Republican Party!"

The conversation loosens up a bit after this little burst of humor. George Shultz and Eduard Shevardnadze both speak. The four men try to come up with a phrase that would encompass the positions of both countries, a sort of lowest common denominator. The idea of a "package agreement" arises, then vanishes, only to reappear on the table later. The ABM Treaty still poses a problem for the Americans, while the Soviets try to understand why Reagan is so attached to his Star Wars. They then review the provisions drafted overnight by the second working group, which oversees human rights issues. This provides Ronald Reagan with an opportunity to attack his counterpart on the lack of "freedom of the press." The Soviet leader dodges the issue. After Shultz's umpteenth attempt to find an acceptable phrasing, Mikhail Gorbachev invites the two sides to take a break. "If the President does not object, we will declare a break until 3 P.M."

The lunch break is a lifesaver, giving both sides a breather and a chance to take stock. The atmosphere is tense on both sides. The Soviets feel like they've staked their all. But their frustration is great. According to them, Ronald Reagan hasn't understood the full extent of their concessions or the historic import of the meeting. On the American side, the president's entourage appears to be divided. Secretary of State Shultz is pushing for an agreement with the Soviets. But Donald Regan and Admiral Poindexter are advising Reagan to stand firm on Star Wars.

## A Tense, Historic Final Round

Three twenty-five that afternoon

The negotiations have started up again, nearly half an hour late. This is the last round, a tight one, with Shevardnadze and Shultz around the table. Mikhail Gorbachev speaks first, pinpointing the problem.

"Concerning the ABM Treaty, I would like to make a proposal which combines your approach and ours. . . . Our formula is as follows: 'The USSR and the U.S. would pledge not to exercise their right to withdraw from the ABM treaty for ten years, and to comply strictly with all its provisions during that period. Testing of all components of ABM defense in space shall be prohibited except for laboratory research and testing. During the first five years of this ten-year period (through 1991), the strategic offensive weapons of the two sides shall be reduced by 50 percent. During the following five years of this period the remaining 50 percent of the two sides' strategic offensive weapons shall be reduced. In this way, by the end of 1996, all the strategic offensive weapons of the USSR and the U.S. will have been eliminated."

The Soviets have come right out with it. Here is a text that both sides can now use as the basis for an accord. Then Ronald Reagan presents the American plan. "Our position offers a somewhat different formulation," he says. "I hope that we can eliminate the difference in the course of our talks."

The American text stipulates: "The two sides agree to limit themselves to research, development, and testing permitted by the ABM Treaty for a period of five years until 1991 inclusive, during which time a 50 percent reduction in strategic nuclear arsenals will be carried out. After that, both sides will continue to reduce the remaining offensive ballistic missiles at the same rate with the aim of completely eliminating offensive ballistic missiles by the end of the second five-year period. The same restrictions in connection with the ABM Treaty will remain in force while the reductions continue at the corresponding rates. At the end of this period, the two sides shall have the right to deploy defensive systems."

Gorbachev seems disappointed with the American formulation. He asserts that it fails "to meet our position halfway." For him, the Americans "are not strengthening" the ABM Treaty during its ten-year period. "What we are talking about primarily is the renunciation of testing any space components of ABM defense in space. . . . I want to emphasize once more that what is prohibited according to our formula does not affect laboratory testing and leaves open the possibility for the American side, like the Soviet side, to conduct any laboratory research relating to space, including SDI research. We are not undermining your idea of SDI. We are permitting that kind of activity, which is already being conducted by the United States and which is impossible to monitor anyway. We are only placing the system within the framework of laboratory research. I think the U.S. could go along with this, especially considering the major steps the Soviet Union has made." He couldn't be any clearer.

Ronald Reagan then shifts the subject to . . . after the ABM Treaty period. "That doesn't remove the question of what we are to do after ten years if we should want to create a defense against ballistic missiles. I just don't understand why you object so much to SDI," he says.

Gorbachev then argues the fact that theoretically there will no longer be any nuclear missiles in ten years. But Reagan brings up a new element: what if someone else, another power, were to start making nuclear missiles? "We want, right now, to provide for the possibility of defense in case, ten years from now, when we no longer have missiles and someone decides to recreate nuclear missiles."

According to Jack Matlock, while the heads of state and their foreign ministers are busy negotiating, a kind of "euphoria" overtakes the advisors waiting behind the scenes in the upstairs rooms. "A barely contained euphoria was beginning to emerge under the emotions on the surface. The United States and the USSR seemed on the point of making the most radical commitment in history to reduce the most destructive weapons known to man," writes Matlock, revealing "exhausted negotiators masking their tension and expectations."

Some digressions ensue in the ground-floor room. The two leaders accuse each other of violating the ABM Treaty since its signing in 1972. Despite the persisting disagreement, Gorbachev insists. "I still wish you would carefully examine our proposal. It encompasses elements of both your and our proposals. If it is acceptable, I am ready to sign it." Shultz then asks for an English version. It will be done, assures the general secretary. Reagan reiterates his fear of a "madman" recreating nuclear missiles after the two superpowers have eliminated their entire arsenals in ten years' time. "I can imagine both of us in ten years getting together again in Iceland to destroy the last Soviet and American missiles under triumphant circumstances," says Reagan, getting carried away. "By then I'll be so old that you won't even recognize me. And you'll ask in surprise: 'Hey, Ron, is that really you? What are you doing here?' And we'll have a big celebration over it."

At which Gorbachev snaps back, "I don't know whether I'll live till that time."

"Well I'm certain I will," replies Reagan.

"Sure you will. You've passed the dangerous age for men, and now you have smooth sailing to be a hundred. But these dangers still lie ahead for me, for a man, they come by the age of sixty and besides I still have to meet with President Reagan, who I can see hates to give in. President Reagan wants to be the winner. But in this case, there can be no winner. Either we both win or we both lose. We're in the same boat."

"I know I won't live to be a hundred if I have to live in fear of these damned missiles," says Reagan.

"Well let's reduce and eliminate them!" counters Gorbachev.

Reagan's Strategic Defense Initiative, the main stumbling block from the start, is now the only issue remaining after two days of discussions. Both sides have come to this same conclusion. Then President Reagan introduces a new idea. "Perhaps we can resolve the matter this way: the question of what research, development and testing are permitted by the ABM Treaty should remain for discussion and negotiation at the meeting in the course of your visit (to the United States). We will come to an agreement regarding the ten-year period and breaking it down into two five-year periods, in the course of which nuclear weapons will be eliminated, while everything having to do with testing, laboratory research and the provisions of the ABM Treaty and so on are things we can discuss at the summit meeting."

Gorbachev is not convinced. "But without that there's no package. All of these issues are interconnected." But Reagan has shifted considerably. At this point, George Shultz steps in. The situation seems frozen. The discussions have reached an impasse and time is running out.

"It seems to me there are two differences between us," begins Shultz. "First, what to consider to be permissible research in the course of the ten-year period. Second, it seems to me, the Soviet side has in mind an indefinitely long period during which we will not be able to withdraw from the ABM Treaty. We have in mind ten years."

Gorbachev answers calmly. "No, we need absolute clarity here." He repeats that the treaty must be enforced and strengthened over the ten-year period. After that, "We will see."

Shultz responds: "In other words, for ten years the two sides will not exercise the right to withdraw from the treaty; after the ten years, this aspect will be gone. Then the sides can exercise that right."

Shevardnadze then adds: "Let me remind you, moreover, that research will not be restricted, but it can only be conducted in the laboratory."

Gorbachev and Shultz resume the dialogue, while Reagan takes a back seat. The American secretary of state asks Gorbachev a number of questions in an effort to clarify the positions on the two sides. In so doing, he is trying to bring the two men closer together.

Shultz wants an agreement. "One question arises which is not a problem, perhaps, but I want to clarify it," he begins. "In your formulation you say that in the course of the following five years the remaining fifty percent of the strategic offensive weapons will be reduced. Do you have in mind a gradual process of reduction which in the long run will lead to the elimination of these weapons by the end of that period?"

Gorbachev responds: "Yes, by the end of the second five-year period they will be completely eliminated."

Shultz: "All right, I understand. But there is another difference. We are talking about the elimination of offensive ballistic missiles."

Gorbachev responds: "But we are already on a 50 percent reduction of all strategic weapons in the course of the first five years. It would be logical for the remaining 50 percent to be eliminated in the following five years. The weapons to be eliminated would include all components of the triad—missiles, including heavy missiles, submarine missiles, and bombers."

## Lost without Nancy and Raisa

After that exchange, in which Secretary of State Shultz clearly seems to want to move closer to the Soviet solution, they take a break. The minutes drag on. Upstairs at Höfdi House, both sides are working on their proposals. At this point, "someone suggests, since Reagan and Gorbachev are tired, that they could prolong the summit for an extra day and let the delegations work overnight on their formulation."

Reagan makes a face and exclaims, "Oh, shit!" recalls advisor Jack Matlock. According to Matlock, Gorbachev and Reagan are both "lost without their wives." In contrast to Raisa, however, Nancy has stayed home in Washington. In the end, no one on the American side is willing to push the proposal all the way. So the summit will end in a few hours as planned. The key question: How might the world have changed if Nancy had come along for the ride?

It's now 5:30 P.M. Back at the negotiating table, Reagan apologizes for being late and says candidly that the American delegation was having "a hard time reaching an agreement." The American president then offers a new text to the Soviets, broadly summarizing what has been discussed so far. Regarding SDI, the main obstacle, the new American formulation is now: "The USSR and the United States undertake for ten years not to exercise their existing right of withdrawal from the ABM Treaty, and during that period strictly to observe all its provisions, while continuing research, development and testing which is permitted by the ABM Treaty."

Naturally, Gorbachev knows immediately where the problem lies. "You speak of research, development and testing which is permitted by the ABM Treaty. Your formulation omits any mention of laboratory testing. Was this done specially?"

At first, Reagan dodges the question, speaking instead about the Geneva Summit. "What I'm asking is did you omit the mention of laboratories deliberately or not?" asks Gorbachev.

"Yes, it was deliberate. What's the matter?" replies Reagan, bordering on provocation. The Soviet leader drops it and says he'll comment later.

Besides the laboratory issue, another misunderstanding suddenly arises regarding the kinds of missiles slated for destruction. Gorbachev doesn't understand why the Americans have referred to strategic offensive missiles for the first five-year period, and to ballistic missiles for the second five-year period.

"Why does the second part of your formulation speak only about ballistic missiles?" Gorbachev asks, since it seems clear to him that all missiles were covered—ground-based, as well as submarine-launched and bombers. "Let me ask this: Do we have in mind—and I think it should be very good—that by the end of the two five-year periods all nuclear explosive devices would be eliminated, including bombs, battlefield systems, cruise missiles, submarine weapons, intermediate-range systems, and so on?" Gorbachev continues enthusiastically, "We could say that, list all the weapons."

Shultz responds: "Then let's do it!" That's one issue settled. All varieties of nuclear missiles are to be eliminated.

A short time later, however, Reagan dampens his secretary of state's enthusiasm. "I do not agree that strict interpretation of the ABM Treaty means restricting the testing of ABM components solely to laboratories," says the American president. "I have already spoken of this. And I have also spoken of the danger of nuclear maniacs."

"Yes, I've heard all about the gas masks and maniacs, probably ten times already," says Gorbachev sarcastically. "But it still does not convince me."

Annoyed, Reagan restates his beliefs. "I'm talking about one possibility of what can happen after ten years. Perhaps there will be nothing of the kind. Perhaps the people who become the leaders at that time will decide that the system is too costly to deploy and will give up SDI."

But the Soviet leader objects again. For him, restricting research to the laboratory "will not mean that the American government will not be able to decide questions relating to the program," he explains, adding firmly that he cannot "allow SDI testing in the atmosphere or in space. That is unacceptable to us. It is a question of principle."

To which Reagan shoots back: "You're destroying all my bridges for continuing SDI. I cannot go along with the restrictions you're demanding."

"With regard to laboratories, is that your final position? If so, we can end our meeting at this point," says Gorbachev dramatically.

Reagan tries to give a detailed explanation. "But you have to understand that experimentation and research cannot always be kept within the laboratory. Sometimes it is simply necessary to go outside the laboratory."

The Soviet leader responds immediately. "You must understand me. To use the laboratory issue is not a matter of stubbornness or hardheadedness. It is all too serious. . . . If you will agree to restrict research work to the laboratory, not letting it out into space, I will be ready in two minutes to sign the appropriate formulation," he says.

Such a document—whether a proper treaty or an outline preparing a future agreement—would be a historical landmark. On this second and final day of negotiations, Gorbachev has staked his all and driven the Americans into a corner. The Soviets are within an inch of securing an agreement stipulating the end of all nuclear weapons after ten years and limiting SDI to laboratory research for the same period.

Secretary of State Shultz seems to be on Gorbachev's side. But there's still one obstacle: Ronald Reagan himself.

"I can't go along with that," the American president responds. "You and I have different positions, different problems. In your country, nobody can criticize you without winding up in prison. In my country, the situation is different. I have a lot of critics who wield great influence. And if I agree to such a formulation, they will launch a campaign against me; they will accuse me of breaking my promise to the people of the United States regarding SDI."

## Emotions Reach a Peak

After nearly two days of nonstop negotiations, the president of the United States has just admitted fearing the reaction of the press, of his opponents, and of the American people if an agreement is reached with the USSR. His doubts are clear in his statement, which he begins by criticizing the lack of freedom in the Soviet Union. Could Ronald Reagan in fact be prepared for an agreement with his Soviet counterpart at this point? Might he be willing to compromise on SDI by restricting it to experimentation in the laboratory for ten years?

Mikhail Gorbachev, a keen judge of character and a brilliant tactician, now tries to get on Reagan's good side. And he plays the moment for dramatic effect. "If I understand you, Mr. President, you are now addressing me in a trusting manner, as a man who occupies in his own country a position equal to yours. Therefore, I say to you frankly and in the same trusting manner: if we sign a package containing major concessions by the Soviet Union regarding fundamental problems, you will become, without exaggeration, a great president. You are now literally two steps from that. If we come to an agreement on strengthening the ABM Treaty and on laboratory research which will not rule out work within the SDI framework, it will mean our meeting has been a success. If not, then let's part at this point and forget about Reykjavík. But there won't be another opportunity like this. At any rate, I know I won't have one."

The Soviet leader pursues his hyperbole, again expressing his main regret, as if already anticipating the summit's failure. "The American side has essentially not made any concessions, not a single major step to meet us halfway. It's hard to do business on that basis."

Then Eduard Shevardnadze speaks up. "Let me speak very emotionally because I feel that we have come very close to accomplishing this historic task. And when future generations read the record of our talks, they will not forgive us if we let this opportunity slip by."

After pausing a few seconds, Ronald Reagan responds. He seems to be hesitating after the emotional charge created by the two Soviets. "Let me say frankly that if I give you what you ask it will definitely hurt me badly at home."

Gorbachev fires back, point-blank: "All right then, let's end it here. What you propose we cannot go along with. I've said all I can."

Reagan challenges him, to which Gorbachev responds: "If I go back to Moscow and say that despite our agreement on deep reductions of nuclear weapons, despite our agreement on the ten-year period, we have given the United States the right to test SDI in space so that the U.S. is ready to deploy it by the end of that period, they will call me a fool and an irresponsible leader."

The two heads of state continue to blame one another for the summit's failure. Reagan returns to the word "laboratory," which has crystallized their hopes and disappointments. "The word 'laboratory' has its own particular meaning and subtext. They would simply tell me in that case that I had capitulated, that I had given away what I promised not to give away," he continues, referring to his "critics" on the domestic front. Then he makes one last try: "I want to ask you once more to change your viewpoint, to do it as a favor to me so that we can go to the people as peacemakers."

Gorbachev refuses. "Even though our meeting is ending this way, I have a clear conscience before my people and before you. I have done everything I could."

"It's too bad we have to part this way." Reagan replies. "We were so close to an agreement. I think you didn't want to achieve an agreement anyway. I'm very sorry."

"I am also very sorry it's happened this way. I wanted an agreement and did everything I could, if not more," responds the Soviet leader.

"I don't know when we'll ever have another chance like this and whether we will meet soon," says Reagan.

"I don't know either," Gorbachev responds, with equal remorse.

## In Hindsight

Emotions have reached a peak when the two leaders say their farewells. It is 6:50 P.M. and the sky over Reykjavík is already dark. It's still drizzling, and they've donned their raincoats.

"It was dark out when we left Höfdi House, and we were all in a foul mood," recalls Gorbachev. Reagan looks distressed as Gorbachev escorts him to his limousine.

"You'd been planning from the beginning to put me in that position," says Reagan, reprimanding Gorbachev as they're standing by their limousines.

"Not at all, Mr. President, I'm ready to go back inside and sign the document regarding all the points we agreed on. Provided that you renounce your plan to weaponize space," declares Gorbachev. "If you change your mind I'm ready to go back inside."

But Reagan doesn't linger, replying simply, "I'm very sorry." Then he gets inside his armored car. Reykjavík is truly over now.

## In Retrospect...

Naturally this episode would have quite an impact. Yet, not everyone shares the same interpretation of what happened behind closed doors at Höfdi House. With time, the protagonists have enlightened us to different degrees. Pavel Palazchenko, one of the official interpreters for Shevardnadze and Gorbachev at Reykjavík, declared after the event that "many on the Soviet side thought that the American SDI program couldn't be stopped, but hoped they could at least limit it and prevent an arms race in space."

Despite having to remain focused to provide the simultaneous translation, Pavel Palazchenko felt, as he expresses it today, that the two sides were "close to a breakthrough. But I also knew very well that even if we reached an agreement in principle, there could be obstacles later. I was realistic. On the second day, though, I felt there were significant issues bringing Reagan and Gorbachev together. They were both disgusted by nuclear weapons. Still, in political terms there were differences. Reagan had his obsession with SDI, and Gorbachev his obsession with the total elimination of nuclear weapons. But deep down they were two simple people who wanted to go as far as they could. Nuclear weapons had to be abolished. Past leaders had basically thought: 'what is a reasonable level of nuclear weapons that we can accept?' But that produced a horrible situation. The Americans alone possessed 30,000 nuclear warheads in their strategic arsenal. Simpler yet more inspired people were needed. It was very important. Otherwise the same thing would have gone on for years."

That said, what prevented Reagan and Gorbachev from reaching an agreement in the end? It's clear from the minutes of their conversations that mistrust was never dropped on either side. Mistrust of the other regime, the other system, and the other ideology. But not only that. For Pavel Palazchenko, the reasons for the mistrust are manifold and nuanced. "For example, at one point the Americans said that after the ten-year period of non-deployment, that deployment could be resumed the next day. As you can imagine, that didn't generate a great deal of trust on the Soviet side. It was completely ridiculous, a total distortion of the whole idea of the ten-year period of total restraint. But for the Americans, it seemed perfectly acceptable. So it was more a question of concrete positions than a lack of trust between the regimes. On the contrary, that lack of trust was already in the process of breaking down. The Geneva Summit had been about the idea of trying to understand one another, that you can't negotiate if there's nothing but mistrust. Our respective positions were no longer based on mistrust by default. People such as Chernyaev, Shevardnadze and Shultz had begun to change their attitude," suggests Palazchenko, who, before being an interpreter, was first and foremost a product of Soviet diplomacy.

For the Russians, Reagan represented the epitome of the right-wing conservative. How could they trust him? "Naturally there was that perception of Reagan. But there was also our perception based on the history of our relations with Richard Nixon in the past," Palazchenko continues. "If you reach an agreement with a conservative American president, you know that it will be ratified and will work. Because he had the authority to unite his side behind his decisions."

The problem was that Reagan wasn't ready to give up his Star Wars vision. "He wanted Gorbachev to agree to SDI," explains Palazchenko. "For him to agree to the overall objective of building an antimissile defense system that would protect the heartland of the United States, and the entire heartland of the Soviet Union. But Gorbachev couldn't agree to linking antimissile defense and offensive strategic weapons. The idea was also that we would reach an agreement on the period of nonwithdrawal from the ABM Treaty. Reagan could very well have agreed to our position and said: 'Well, I protected SDI, we're going to plan a program of research, do some testing, and we'll continue to preserve my dream'. . . That wouldn't have been a problem. We could have very easily 'choreographed' that." Palazchenko sighs with regret.

In fact, it is far from certain that a practical SDI system could have been achievable in ten years. Palazchenko even says that according to one Soviet nuclear expert, physicist Evgeny Velikhov, SDI "would be extremely difficult to achieve from a technical point of view, and impossible from a cost/benefit standpoint."

Roald Sagdeev has put forward a different view of the disagreement around SDI. For this physicist and advisor to Gorbachev on nuclear issues, the stumbling block regarding SDI development in a laboratory or in space could have been sidestepped. Sagdeev wasn't present in Iceland because the Soviet leader's entourage had been severely reduced. But he was certainly in Geneva in 1985 and took part in the preparatory meetings for Reykjavík. "We knew the grace period would probably be agreed to," he says, referring to the ten-year application of the ABM Treaty with no right of withdrawal. "But we didn't know that Reagan would make such a dramatic proposal—to eliminate all strategic nuclear forces. And many of his advisors didn't know it either. It came out of nowhere! Gorbachev was impressed," he recalls.

For the scientist, who was in favor of an agreement with the Americans, Reykjavík remains a "historic missed opportunity." But contrary to what one might expect from a former Soviet official, he doesn't think the fault lies with Ronald Reagan, but rather with Mikhail Gorbachev. The whole debate over the word "laboratory" seems almost laughable to him today. Or the debate missed the point, at any rate. "Gorbachev himself didn't understand everything they were talking about," asserts Sagdeev.

The physicist then recounts this telling anecdote. "A day or two after they returned to Moscow, I had a call from Shevardnadze. He says, 'Can you come in and see me?' So I go to his office and he says: 'I have a question. I don't understand when Gorbachev was talking about a laboratory. What does it mean?" It was clear to me that Shevardnadze was also highly disappointed after Reykjavík. Otherwise he wouldn't have asked me that. I said, "'You know, if you read *Pravda* the day after the first cosmonaut was launched into orbit, it says: a great step forward, enlarging the space laboratory.'"

"The term 'laboratory' doesn't mean someone sitting in a little room in the basement," continued Sagdeev to the minister of foreign affairs. "Space is also a laboratory. It means 'experimentation.' What's different is the scope of the experimentation and what is brought into outer space."

In short, they could have experimented in space, but not necessarily on a large scale and only under certain conditions.

"Shevardnadze was relieved and said, 'Professor, can you go to New York and speak before the United Nations to explain your version of laboratories?' I said all right. He said, 'Can you go tomorrow?' In 24 hours I got a diplomatic passport and a few days later I was in New York, hosted by the Soviet mission to the UN. They had a little VIP hotel inside their embassy. I spoke and explained. The next day, the headlines in *The New York Times* and *The Washington Post* read: 'Soviet Official Admits Space is a Laboratory, Too.' Shevardnadze was disappointed in Gorbachev."

It's a short step from there to imagining there was a misunderstanding at Höfdi House over the definition of the word 'laboratory.' But Sagdeev doesn't take that step. He responds in another way. "I don't think either Gorbachev or Reagan had any precise understanding of it." According to Sagdeev, the Soviet side was divided over the issue of agreeing to SDI research and development. But their internal disagreements didn't come out at Reykjavík. "It was Shevardnadze and people close to Gorbachev who sent me to issue that statement in New York. And there were others who didn't like it. What's clear is that the Politburo was divided," he recalls today.

Roald Sagdeev is talkative. At eighty-two years old, he takes pleasure in looking back on these historic moments. His eyes that sparkle with laughter are penetrating behind his slightly old-fashioned glasses with their rectangular frames. He continues with another anecdote dating back to when the

Soviet delegation returned from Reykjavík. "Georgy Arbatov, an advisor to Gorbachev, asked to see me. He said, 'You know, Roald, I have to tell you, when I was at the Kremlin I ran into Viktor Chebrikov, a member of the Politburo and head of the KGB. He came over and said: 'We know you're a friend of Sagdeev. We respect him, he's a good scientist. But you should tell him that he sometimes comes out with bad statements,'" referring to the laboratory remark at UN headquarters. "It wasn't so much a threat as friendly advice," says Sagdeev, smiling.

But then, what could have been acceptable to the two leaders with respect to SDI? Was there room for a different formulation? A different principle? Reagan and Gorbachev didn't go into the technical details of launching missiles and lasers in orbit. "Perhaps their technical advisors could have helped them," Sagdeev says thoughtfully. "But there clearly wasn't much scientific credibility around SDI. Then why was Gorbachev so afraid of it?" he wonders.

And yet, the general secretary of the CPSU was surrounded by advisors, including technical experts such as Sagdeev and Velikhov. "But there were also conservatives saying, 'Let's do our own SDI, better and cheaper,'" says Sagdeev, putting things in perspective. "I was at one of those meetings. The missiles minister said to Gorbachev, 'Michael Sergeyovitch, why waste all this time? Let's do our own program, much better and cheaper.' Those guys were dangerous. But to me it was an aberration. Technically, it couldn't work. And I think Gorbachev knew that it wouldn't work."

According to Jack Matlock, Reagan's European affairs advisor and notetaker during most of the sessions in Reykjavík, Gorbachev was also to blame. In any event, he quotes Marshal Akhromeyev, speaking to Reagan's special advisor Paul Nitze as they were leaving on Sunday evening: "It's not my fault." In short, the military man was trying to pass the buck for Gorbachev's obstinacy onto the civilians. And probably onto the Kremlin chief himself.

But then why did the Soviet leader push so hard for strictly limiting SDI to a conventional, earthbound laboratory? "Indeed, Gorbachev knew that SDI wouldn't work. So why hold the summit? Knowing that, he was angry. Gorbachev wanted to be right all the time. In my opinion, that's the reason" the discussions failed, Sagdeev believes today. "It wasn't logical to push for that. But Gorbachev gave the Americans the impression that he was afraid of SDI, just because he talked about it a lot and because he wanted to be right . . . His temperament got the upper hand over politics."

Sagdeev sums up the story in one phrase: "The Americans oversold the Strategic Defense Initiative and the Russians overbought it."

"Naturally we were all disappointed when the extraordinary breakthroughs we had hoped for were not realized," confirms George Shultz.

President Reagan himself was disappointed, recalls John Poindexter: "He was disappointed with Gorbachev. Not with himself. Well, he was disappointed with himself for not bringing Gorbachev to his position."

"Yet any immediate disappointment faded quickly as it was clear that enormous progress had been made," continues George Shultz. "The things we had agreed upon—intermediate-range missiles and reducing strategic weapons—were fully developed subsequently, and the agreement according to which human rights would be part of regular discussions was a prelude to major changes."

# EIGHT

# *From Hangover to START*

S tunned. While American and Soviet delegations slowly prepare to leave Höfdi, under the drizzle, the night already falling, both leaders look like boxers who'd each lost the match. But the champions of each half of a divided world will not react the same way publicly. The Russian side will present itself as united and on the offensive. On the American side, faces register visible defeat. And that evening three characters, short-circuited and each contradicting the other, reveal a team deeply divided: those in favor of a historic agreement and those opposed. With at least one side so at odds, generating any post-Reykjavík condominium will be painful.

But patiently, Americans and Soviets will resume the dialogue to arrive at a Strategic Arms Reduction Treaty (START) that will be signed in 1990, after the departure of Ronald Reagan from the presidency.

## The Misfortunes of George Shultz

As Reagan heads to the US Air Force base in Keflavík to pay tribute to the airmen stationed in Iceland before returning to Washington, the secretary of state gives a press conference. For many of his colleagues, the appearance of George Shultz this evening is bordering on the catastrophic. For the rest of the world, it will reveal the extent of the damage—the failure of an agreement that should have been historic, ushering the world into a new era.

"Of course, we were all disappointed that the extraordinary breakthroughs could not be realized," George Shultz recalls today. "But all immediate disappointments quickly disappeared, as it was clear that immense progress had been made." That evening, however, the face of the head of American diplomacy says more than all the speeches. The man appears haggard as he goes before the world's press, exhausted by the two-day marathon discussion, devastated by how close they came to an agreement that would have led toward the elimination of all nuclear weapons on the planet in ten years.

Shultz wears a dark suit and a sky blue shirt, accented with a burgundy tie. On the small platform of the narrow press room in

Reykjavík, he stands in front of a blue background, an American flag on his right. The secretary of state begins to speak, NBC broadcasting live this performance of a man who takes full blame for the results at Reykjavík and who now feels obliged to account for his failure—or that of his boss.

George Shultz speaks slowly. He is choosing his words with the greatest care in his ten-minute opening statement. He talks about "potential agreement," or "agreement that could have been found" without going into details, leaving the journalists in his audience hungering for any substance. "At the end, with great reluctance, the president . . . simply had to refuse to compromise the security of the United States, its allies and freedom. We are deeply disappointed by this outcome," he concludes, his features drawn.

The performance of this chief of American diplomacy must be given some considerable weight. After having invested himself so deeply in the discussions, desperate for some positive outcome, he has still found it impossible to compose himself. George Shultz is a man utterly wasted. He is aware of the historical opportunity that he played a central, though clearly not defining, role in. Above all, this press conference helps us understand today how deeply the American delegation was divided. Shultz and his diplomats were clearly in favor of an agreement with the Soviets. The soldiers, led by Poindexter, were much less so.

"Shultz was in mourning for his entire press conference," says Patrick Buchanan, who was a member of the American delegation at Reykjavík. "There was a lot of emotion in the American delegation, especially after the failure. But frankly, I was pretty happy." But Buchanan quickly qualifies himself. "I do not mean to speak too badly of him, but I do not think Shultz served the cause well. He let his personal emotions take precedence over reality. Perhaps he wanted an agreement at all costs. . . . But it was a bad deal."

John Poindexter, the national security advisor, also watched the live broadcast of George Shultz from a corner of the press room. Like Buchanan, he was most critical of the secretary of state's performance. "Shultz was very disappointed. In fact, people felt that this press conference itself was a disaster. Don [Regan] and I were looking at each other, and I was amazed at how Shultz was talking about it. I was very discouraged. It left a terrible impression on the media," he said recently in an interview.

## Gorbachev on the Podium

In Reykjavík, journalists had not been briefed during the talks on the content of the negotiations in Höfdi, the summit being held *in camera*. So, while listening to Shultz speak, they seem to take in, little by little, a measure of the historical dimension of the failure. Shultz describes only in outline the nature of the talks, justifying Reagan's position without explaining how far the discussions had gone toward the goal of total elimination of nuclear weapons in ten years.

If the Americans appear divided, the Soviet camp leaves no room for doubt. It is Mikhail Gorbachev himself who speaks that evening in Reykjavík in front of a crowd of incredulous journalists. And the Soviet leader does not dither. He understands that he must now win the public relations battle.

"I had about forty minutes before the scheduled press conference," he recalls in his book, *Mémoirs*. "I had only one desire: to stigmatize the American position. . . . Yet, while walking [toward the venue], a thought bothered me: we had succeeded in reaching an agreement on strategic and intermediate missiles, which created a new situation. . . . When I entered the enormous hall of the press center where nearly a thousand journalists were waiting for the Soviet delegation, I had not yet made a definitive decision. I was suddenly seized by a profound emotion—the thought that all these people who faced me represented the human race waiting for its fate to be decided. This upset me. It was at this moment that I understood the scope of what had just happened in Reykjavík and what we had to do."

So, in a long tirade, the general secretary of the Communist Party attacks. He accuses Ronald Reagan, placing on him all the responsibility for an historic failure. Gorbachev delivers his speech at almost the same time as George Shultz. His words slice through the atmosphere. The master of the Kremlin appears powerfully in charge. He succeeds in distilling, gradually, several elements in his successful effort to condemn the attitude of the Americans—the first glimpse the press has had of the detailed content of the discussions that had just concluded in Höfdi House.

After recalling that the Reykjavík Summit had taken place on his initiative, Gorbachev sets the stage. "The atmosphere was friendly. We had the opportunity to present our views freely and without restriction," he begins. "This has allowed us to deepen our understanding of the world's major political problems, bilateral relations, those issues that have the world's attention, the problems of war and peace, and the end of the nuclear arms race. And all the complexities of these issues. I suggested to President [Reagan] that here in Reykjavík we give instructions to our foreign ministers and relevant departments [to begin working toward] three rough drafts of agreements that the president and I could sign later, during my visit to the United States of America."

The Soviet leader then lists the topics of these draft agreements: "strategic weapons, intermediate-range missiles, and the question of verification" of the first two points. Gorbachev continues to elaborate to the assembled journalists, his account of the discussions, unveiling the 50 percent reduction of strategic weapons over five years and then a total elimination in ten years. Also, the agreement to exclude intermediate missiles in Europe and Asia from cutbacks of the two superpowers. For him, it is a question of justifying himself and showing that the Soviets made any number of concessions.

Then he goes on the attack. Turning to the ABM Treaty, he no longer restrains himself from attacking the Americans. Since

AN IMPOSSIBLE DREAM

"we were prepared to make deep cuts in nuclear weapons, we had to ask the question: as soon as we enter the concrete phase of the elimination of nuclear weapons we must be absolutely clear on the question of verification. The audit must now become stricter. The Soviet Union is in favor of triple-checking, which would allow both parties to feel perfectly confident that this will not lead to a trap. We reaffirmed that we were prepared for all forms of verification. This issue has also been included in our position. . . . If we settle on the practical abolition of nuclear weapons, another problem arises. Each party must have a guarantee that the other side will no longer seek military superiority. I think this is a perfectly fair and legitimate demand, from a political point of view and from a military point of view. . . . That is why we raised the following question: If we were to approach the phase of real, profound reductions, in ten years—and this is how we see it—all nuclear capabilities in the United States and the Soviet Union would be eliminated. In this case, it would be necessary to ensure that during this period the mechanisms of limiting the arms race, particularly the ABM Treaty, above all, would not be weakened, but strengthened. Our proposal may therefore be summarized as follows: the parties should strengthen the ABM Treaty, a treaty of limited duration, with a firm commitment not to withdraw from the treaty for a period of ten years. . . . We have also indicated that all the obligations of the ABM Treaty must be fulfilled in these ten years and that only research and anti-missile tests under

189

laboratory conditions would be authorized. . . . We are aware of the commitment of the administration and the President to the Strategic Defense Initiative. We agreed to continue laboratory testing, which would give the President the opportunity to refine his ideas and then clarify what exactly SDI is. . . . We were about to make major and historic decisions. . . . Instructions were needed to draft the treaties and to work on the procedures to be applied. It could have been signed during my visit to Washington. But the American side has torpedoed all this. . . . I think, however, that the encounter as a whole, here, has major significance. After all, we were close to agreeing. We only failed to formalize it. . . . The path we have taken to reach this agreement on a major reduction of nuclear weapons here in Iceland has given us substantial experience and we have made considerable progress."

Meanwhile, Ronald Reagan is talking to the GIs stationed in Iceland, at the Keflavík air base, who have no idea what is happening just a few miles away. "Thank you all. It's good to feel at home," he begins. "Let me first say that the discussions I had with General Secretary Gorbachev were encouraging and helpful. We talked at length about arms control, a subject of vital importance to the world, and human rights and regional conflicts. Of course, General Secretary Gorbachev and I were frank about our disagreements, many of which remain. But we laid a foundation for what could be a successful summit in the United States in the future."

This represents the first reaction of the president of the United States, who has scheduled a televised address to the American people the next day—an address that, as expected, would say nothing negative. But his legendary optimism seems to be catching up with him, as he talks about a future summit in the United States—that has yet to be fixed.

## Stunned in Air Force One

Following Reagan's brief statement to the troops, the Gorbachev offensive, and especially the negative effect of the George Shultz press conference, other members of the American delegation begin to react. Onboard Air Force One, Admiral Poindexter goes to the back of the aircraft. While he usually speaks off the record to journalists accredited to the White House, this time the national security advisor allows them to quote him—proof of the importance of the event. There follows a surrealistic dialogue as the leading American correspondents realized little by little what had happened a few hours earlier in Iceland. Or rather, what almost happened.

From the outset, Poindexter tries to limit expectations. "As we said before coming here, we really did not expect any agreement [with the Soviets]," he begins, then continues, telling the reporters about intermediate-range missiles and the problem of nuclear testing. But the press asks him very quickly about SDI. In order to carry out the full-scale tests, not in the laboratory, "the ABM treaty would remain in place, but there would be a new treaty with provisions that would conflict with the ABM treaty," he tries to explain. The American plan was a sincere effort to find a solution that would enable both countries to make the transition from a situation where each depend on offensive weapons for strategic deterrence to a situation where each could depend on defensive systems to maintain deterrence. In other words, no longer to count on offensive missiles to defend themselves, but on a system of defense, or Star Wars.

Then the doyenne of the White House press corps, Helen Thomas of United Press International (UPI) asks: "Why are the Soviets so afraid of SDI? Then she adds: "Is it about a pre-emptive strike? Is it because they want time to catch up with us or are they really afraid of being destroyed?"

"That's a big question, Helen, and I do not know how to answer it," says the national security advisor. Behind the cameras, other questions follow. "Do you think they have mastered this technology? You say that we are very close to getting there. Do they think we are so close?" Sadly, the admiral replies that "SDI is not around the corner. I do not want you to think we've had some sort of [technological] breakthrough." He adds that future negotiations would take place, but that no date had been set by the two delegations. Then Admiral Poindexter tells the reporters he wants to make "a little remark."

"As you will see in a moment, Gorbachev has held hostage all the weapons control agreements that both parties had prepared."

ABOVE: Titan 2 Missile in its silo, at the Titan Missile Museum in Sahuarita, Arizona. BELOW: Control Room for the Titan 2 Missile silo, at the Titan Missile Museum in Sahuarita, Arizona. *Both photographs from Guillaume Serina.*

ABOVE: Ronald Reagan greets Mikhail Gorbachev inside Hofdi House in Reykjavik, Iceland, on October 11, 1986. BELOW: The two leaders meet outside Hofdi House on October 11, 1986, in front of the international press, before the start of the negotiation. *Both photographs from the National Archives/Ronald Reagan Presidential Library.*

ABOVE: Ronald Reagan confers with his advisers during a break on the second day of the negotiations, on October 12, 1986. George Shultz, Donald Regan and John Poindexter can be seen. BELOW: The two leaders have a brief talk inside Hofdi House, in front of the cameras, on that first morning. *Both photographs from the National Archives/Ronald Reagan Presidential Library.*

ABOVE: The first one-on-one discussion on October 11, 1986, in Hofdi House. Only two interpreters are present. BELOW: Second day of negotiations on October 12, 1986. Eduard Shevardnadze (the Soviet Foreign Affairs Minister) and George Shultz (the American Secretary of State) are present, along the two interpreters including Pavel Palazchenko. *Both photographs from the National Archives/Ronald Reagan Presidential Library.*

Ronald Reagan and his advisers on the second day. *From the National Archives/Ronald Reagan Presidential Library.*

Ronald Reagan is back in the United States on October 12, 1986. He is greeted by First Lady Nancy Reagan at Andrews Air Force Base. *From the National Archives/Ronald Reagan Presidential Library.*

ABOVE: Mikhail Gorbachev back in front of Hofdi House in Reykjavik in 2006. *From Pavel Palazchenko/Gorbachev Foundation.* BELOW: Guillaume Serina meets Mikhail Gorbachev in Moscow in 2015. *From Guillaume Serina.*

ABOVE: Tosh and Yorie Kano, Hiroshima survivors with Guillaume Serina at the Hiroshima Peace Memorial Park, in Japan, on May 27, 2016. RIGHT: U.S. President Barack Obama and Japan's Prime Minister Shinzo Abe at the Hiroshima Peace Memorial Park, in Japan, on May 27, 2016. Barack Obama was the first sitting president to visit the site and pay tribute to the victims of the first atomic bomb. *Both photographs from Guillaume Serina.*

A reporter asks, "They are all linked?"

"All of them," Poindexter replies. A short time later, after reminding journalists of the different types of missiles, Reagan's advisor reiterates that Gorbachev would have "linked SDI and arms reductions. We knew that's what he planned to do, but last night they also linked arms reductions, INF intermediate missiles and nuclear tests into a single agreement including the ABM Treaty." One way to summarize the negotiations a bit hastily, if not entirely falsely.

As the improvised press conference advances, more journalists ask for details. Despite their fatigue, the protagonists of this conversation go on the offensive and are deeply concerned about the details. One journalist asks Poindexter to repeat some issues with technical precision, another, running out of tape for his recorder, feverishly asks a colleague for a new cassette. Poindexter continues to justify the lack of an historic agreement. He emphasizes the difference in the interpretation of the ABM Treaty.

Another question from a reporter: "So, in the end, all this was based on the definition of the ABM Treaty—the broad vision versus the narrow vision?

"No, that's not quite right," Poindexter explains patiently. "It is not simply the difference between a broad or narrow interpretation, they [the Soviets] want to make it narrower. They want to make it more restrictive by limiting research, development and testing of any system in space to the laboratory."

One journalist seizes the floor and sums up the situation: "Let me synthesize. It all goes back to the fact that the president did not want to give up on SDI. Was SDI the most important thing for them?"

"No, that's not true," replies Poindexter.

"Well, SDI is what has caused everything to fall apart," the journalist says.

"But it is not true that we do not want to give up anything," said the admiral. "We—the president—agreed we were ready to suspend the SDI deployment for ten years."

"But the president does not even have SDI. He [Reagan] will not have it until about eleven years."

"It's not necessarily the case."

"But SDI is really the central point," concludes the journalist.

The dialogue continues between the correspondents and the advisor. Most of the time on the record, with some asides off the record. If what Poindexter says during these "background" moments is quoted in an article, then he will have to be designated as a White House official, not by his name, nor his function. At the end of this long briefing, Poindexter confirms that SDI is a kind of "insurance policy" in case of non-compliance by the Soviets with the agreements to destroy nuclear weapons. So, the failure of the negotiations was "based on the definition of SDI."

"They wanted to restrict (SDI) to the laboratory, which is more restrictive than the existing treaty, even more restrictive than any narrow interpretation. We, and in particular the

President—and I agree with him—thought it would kill the SDI program."

Immediately after the end of this press briefing, *Time* reporter Hugh Sidey writes a pool dispatch to be relayed to all journalists and their media, on behalf of all the reporters on board Air Force One. Sidey describes the national security adviser as "dark, tired, but happy to explain the events that perplexed everyone at Reykjavík." Sidey points out that the briefing aboard Air Force One lasted "an hour and twenty minutes. . . . Poindexter first perching on a chair, then sitting on a stool, elbows placed on a table. He was without a tie . . . and, clearly, he needed rest." A precise account, faithfully summing up what was said over the previous two days, follows this report, stressing that "Sunday was crucial."

This press briefing by the admiral aboard the presidential plane has a dual purpose: it not only counterbalances the negative impression left by George Shultz a few hours earlier, but also serves to open a sequence of aggressive communications from the White House. It is out of the question to pass for the losers, responsible for the summit's failure. As a result, the entire Reagan machine is moving into high gear and, starting on Monday, will try to give a much more positive spin to the events in Reykjavík—even if it means easing away from the truth. From Monday through Wednesday, October 13 to 15, the sequence is clearly political and purely for domestic consumption. After all, the American midterm elections are just two weeks away.

## Bring on the Spin Doctors

The following day, Monday, October 13, George Shultz is in Brussels at NATO headquarters to meet with the foreign ministers of the Atlantic Alliance. It is noon, and following the session, he faces down the journalists of the European countries—allies of the United States. They try to understand what really happened in Reykjavík the previous day and the day before. The secretary of state, for his part, tries to correct the defeatist impression he had left during his earlier press conference.

"Today I had the opportunity to describe in detail the process and content of the Reykjavík meetings to my NATO counterparts, and each of them was able to express his views." Shultz begins. "I was struck, as always during our meetings, by the cohesion, the constructive tone of our discussions."

After this start, which amounts to little more than double-talk, the assembled journalists bear down on the secretary. Unlike the previous day, Shultz struggles to be positive, and at the same time, more aggressive towards the Soviets. By this time, the White House is already trying to recover from the harsh blow dealt by the collapse of the talks and develop a coherent strategy towards the media and public opinion—above all, not to demonstrate any of the dissension that may have marked the internal dynamics of the American delegation in Reykjavík. For Patrick Buchanan, director of communications at the White House, this is not really about damage control. "You can call it damage control," he says today, "but that was not the case since, in my opinion, the president had made the right choice."

Back in the White House West Wing, it's battle stations. President Reagan is set to address the nation that evening on television. He is inundated with suggestions on the tone and content for his speech. George Shultz, in Europe, sends his reflections. "We should look at Iceland as a major phase in moving towards a more secure and stable world." Then he tries to influence directly the tone the president should use with his audience.

"I hope your tone will be constructive rather than aggressive and geared towards future opportunities," Shultz writes. "Your important ideas are still on the table," he says, and insists on the constructive aspects of the Reykjavík discussions. After three paragraphs, he comes around to SDI, as if to cut the legs out from under his critics. "We launched SDI—the key to a world without nuclear weapons."

When he receives these notes, Ronald Reagan is in the Oval Office. He is personally overseeing the writing of his speech—an occurrence rare enough to underline its importance. Usually, the president has a team of speechwriters, led by his extraordinary chief speechwriter, Peggy Noonan, who had been plucked early in the Reagan administration from her role as writer of Dan Rather's radio commentaries at CBS News. In most cases, the president would add a few of his own modifications, adapting it to his own speech patterns. But this time, on October 13, Reagan himself puts his words on paper—five dense pages in tightly worded handwriting. He knows that the stakes are enormous—not only with the midterm elections coming up in just two weeks, but also with his credibility as leader of the free world.

"Good evening. I am sure that most of you know, I have just returned from Iceland, where the General Secretary of the Soviet Union, Gorbachev, had invited me," he begins. Throughout the text, corrections, erasures, clarifications, and comments appear—most provided by his White House advisors. Clearly, Reagan wants to deliver a speech that matters.

At 8:00 P.M. Eastern Time, all the major television networks have cleared their prime-time schedules to broadcast the speech live. Reagan is sitting behind his desk in the Oval Office. Behind him are photos of his wife Nancy and their family. His features drawn, his face serious, the old actor reads from a teleprompter as the words scroll slowly upward. He is looking the American people directly in their eyes. In case of a breakdown, he has the same text on his desk before him printed in large uppercase characters. He holds it in his hands and, discreetly, when the prompter indicates, he moves the completed page to his right. The President wears a black suit, white shirt, and dark red tie. He will talk for twenty minutes.

"Good evening. As most of you know, I have just returned from several meetings in Iceland with the leader of the Soviet

Union, General Secretary Gorbachev. As I did last year when I returned from the summit conference in Geneva, I want to take a few moments tonight to share with you what took place in these discussions," he says in measured tones. "The implications of these talks are enormous and only just beginning to be understood." Then, he sets out effectively the "American version" of the Reykjavík Summit—an artificial, somewhat biased presentation of the real negotiations.

"We proposed the most sweeping and generous arms control proposal in history. We offered the complete elimination of all ballistic missiles—Soviet and American—from the face of the Earth by 1996. While we parted company with this American offer still on the table, we are closer than ever before to agreements that could lead to a safer world without nuclear weapons." As can be seen, the president of the United States interprets the facts to his interest. He says the initiative came entirely from the Americans.

Reagan then puts on the face of the great communicator, as he is known to the American people. Like a high-school instructor, he explains slowly and carefully the abbreviations ABM and SDI. He accuses the Soviets directly of not having played fair under the ABM Treaty, even "violating" it with the construction of a radar facility in Krasnoyarsk, "which we believe is a critical part of a radar system designed to provide radar guidance for antiballistic missiles protecting the entire nation. Now, this is a violation of the ABM Treaty." The president turns then to SDI, calling it an "insurance policy."

"Let me make it clear, SDI is a non-nuclear defense," he says. He recalls, as he had done two days earlier in Reykjavík, the possibility of a "madman deciding to create nuclear missiles," adding "I liken it to our keeping our gas masks even though the nations of the world had outlawed poison gas after World War I." Reagan now faithfully summarizes the ten-year proposal to eliminate nuclear arsenals, but his interpretation of the failure does not coincide entirely with reality.

"And here the debate began," Reagan says. "The general secretary wanted wording that, in effect, would have kept us from developing the SDI for the entire ten years. In effect, he was killing SDI. And unless I agreed, all that work toward eliminating nuclear weapons would go down the drain—canceled. I told him I had pledged to the American people that I would not trade away SDI, there was no way I could tell our people their government would not protect them against nuclear destruction. I went to Reykjavík determined that everything was negotiable except two things: our freedom and our future. I'm still optimistic that a way will be found. The door is open, and the opportunity to begin eliminating the nuclear threat is within reach."

This is the most questionable part of Reagan's assertions. Nowhere in his address to the nation does he invoke the word "laboratory." He never says that Gorbachev agreed to ten years of SDI testing in the laboratory, but not in space. He prefers to accuse the Soviets of a rigidity at odds with their real position.

The balance of the president's message dealt with his view of the world and his vision of America's place in it, invoking America's commitment to "the extension of freedom," and drawing "the moral distinctions between totalitarianism and democracy." A good way to justify his position during the negotiations. Moreover, he even points out that "the Soviets understand" that "SDI is the key to a world without nuclear weapons. They have devoted far more resources, for a lot longer time than we, to their own SDI. The world's only operational missile defense today surrounds Moscow, the capital of the Soviet Union." A two-part assertion, the first part of which, as we have seen, is far from verified, and the second of which is specifically permitted by the ABM Treaty already in force.

Reagan's conclusion is intended to be solemn, the most important message for any great communicator, and the one his audience must retain. "Another president, Harry Truman, noted that our century has seen two of the most frightful wars in history and that 'the supreme need of our time is for man to learn to live together in peace and harmony.' It's in pursuit of this ideal I went to Geneva a year ago and to Iceland last week. And it's in pursuit of that ideal that I thank you now for all the support you've given me, and I ask for your help and your prayers as we continue our journey toward a world where peace reigns and freedom is enshrined. Thank you, and God bless you."

The next day, Tuesday, October 14, the White House advisors are doing the after-sales service calls—reinforcing the explanations of the day before. Several meetings take place with the press, on several levels. The president himself goes to the White House's Roosevelt Room at 1:26 P.M. to meet with the anchors of the nation's television networks and the most influential commentators. He's followed a half an hour later by his chief of staff, Donald Regan, accompanied by Patrick Buchanan, the director of communications. National Security Council member Jack Matlock does the same a little later. Richard Perle, who was a member of the delegation in Iceland, represents the Defense Department and briefs the Pentagon press the same day.

For the most part, American journalists are calling for clarification—trying to trace the exact chronology of events in Reykjavík, to understand how the two leaders could fail to agree. At their on-the-record conversation with the president, the journalists wonder if Gorbachev had been lying. The word "duplicity" is suggested. Others confront the president: "When it appeared that the general secretary was ready to make all these concessions on offensive armaments that were linked directly with SDI, did not you feel that you had a chance to reply, 'We will come back to you. We will study this with our experts?' If you had that option, you very clearly did not choose it."

Another editorial writer remarked: "But you say, Mr. President, that he left you no choice but to say yes or no on the spot, and that you did not have a chance to say, 'Very interesting, we will study it and we will come back to you?'"

"There was no need for that," Reagan replies tersely. "In no way would I distance myself from that, from SDI."

The press is worried about the future. Will negotiations at a lower level, between diplomats, resume in Geneva? How will the European allies readjust their positions? And will there be, as expected, a summit in Washington? And if so, where and when will they resume the conversation?

This total media effort begins to bear fruit. An NBC/*Wall Street Journal* poll, which the White House previews on October 15 before its publication, encourages the administration. Some 72 percent of Americans surveyed believe the president "did the right thing" by holding on to SDI. To the question: "Would you vote for a congressman who supports the president about SDI?" Some 53 percent reply "yes" and 38 percent, "no." In another poll of a thousand people on October 13 and 14, 20 percent believe Reykjavík was a defeat for nuclear disarmament, and 78 percent do not think so. Only 2 percent have no opinion.

The press is, on the whole, critical. The political class as well. In the days that follow, Democrats—the majority party in the House of Representatives, though the Republicans hold the Senate—unload on the president and his actions in Reykjavík. "The only way that Star Wars will become an object of negotiation for future generations is if Congress comes back next year with an axe," said Democratic representative Ed Markey.

On October 16, Massachusetts senator Edward M. Kennedy, brother of President Kennedy who faced down Nikita

Khrushchev over nuclear missiles in the Cuban Missile Crisis, puts Reagan's actions in historical perspective. Writing in a *New York Times* Op-Ed column, "It is difficult to believe that any other President since World War II would have ignored the opportunity that knocked in Reykjavík."

Patrick Leahy, Vermont's Democratic senator tells his home-town newspaper, the *Rutland Herald*, that "negotiations have failed because of the government's commitment to a system that does not exist. They seem to ignore that the Soviet nuclear warheads are real. I must admit that I do not understand this logic." Democratic representative Berkley Bedell of Iowa, who had co-sponsored with Republican colleague Jim Leach a reso-lution urging test-ban negotiations, warns the House: "The US delegation went to Iceland empty-handed and returned to the United States empty-handed and confused."

Another particularly eminent voice of the Democratic party was Jimmy Carter, Reagan's predecessor in the White House who'd lost to Reagan in the November 1980 elections. In the *Atlanta Journal and Constitution* on October 18, he spoke clearly of a "big mistake."

"I do not think they [the Reagan administration] were prepared for what Gorbachev wanted to put on the table of proposals going so far," continuing, "I always thought that Star Wars was a big mistake. My judgment is that President Reagan has missed a very good opportunity." He also mentions that the White House had reached out to him by phone during the

Reykjavík weekend while he was traveling in Michigan. It was "one of the few times in five and a half years" that he was consulted by his successor's team. But Carter does not divulge the content of the conversation. Carter says only that he is confident "Reagan wanted a reduction agreement only on intermediate missiles and that he was keeping himself from the more spectacular agreements [in hopes of achieving] a politically popular summit" in the United States.

The foreign, particularly the European, press turns harshly against the American president. On Monday, the day after Reykjavík, the US Information Agency, a state department unit in Washington that monitors global coverage of the United States and relays government news abroad, issues a first report on global reaction to Reykjavík, which is immediately reported to the White House.

"The world media summed up the meeting between the president and Gorbachev as 'a failure' and speculated on the low probability of a summit between the superpowers in the United States this year," the USIA report begins. Continent by continent, the titles and comments of editorial writers, reporters, and editors are methodically indexed. America's allies, particularly in Europe, are especially important to Washington.

*The London Times* singles out President Reagan directly: "The Reykjavík summit ended in a stalemate yesterday after President Reagan's refusal to accept any limit on his Star Wars research program. . . . Mr. Shultz, dark and defeated, said the

United States was 'deeply disappointed' by this outcome." *The Financial Times* raises an alarm: "The failure of leaders to produce the slightest agreement, even on a future summit, could be a significant setback for East-West relations," writes correspondent Patrick Cockburn.

In France, whose government had criticized SDI, notably in a letter from the French ambassador to the Reagan administration, the Radio France correspondent in Washington, Jean-Luc Hees, says, "George Shultz, who was responsible for the failed political outcome, is one of the main victims of the weekend." The center-right French daily *Le Figaro* analyzes the situation from the Soviet perspective: "Gorbachev's insistence on abandoning SDI has dispelled the ambiguities created by the Soviet leader's seductive campaign to win over American and European opinion. But Gorbachev's veto is also a way of showing the world that Reagan is a warlike leader."

The German newspaper *Die Welt*, on its front page, emphasizes that Reykjavík's failure "does not mean that the negotiations on disarmament in Geneva stop there. However, the task of both delegations in the coming weeks and months will be to do away with the debris left over from the Icelandic summit . . . [which] will expose Reagan to sharp criticism from those who warned him not to accept Gorbachev's invitation to Iceland. Everything indicates that the Soviets will exploit the failure of the summit by launching a new propaganda campaign." The *Frankfurter Allgemeine Zeitung* newspaper goes further, saying that "the Soviets scored points thanks to their controlled performance," suggesting, of course, that Reagan was out of control.

## In Moscow, Another Vision

The Soviet press on Monday, October 13, proves once again that it is directly guided by the Kremlin, even the Politburo. "Can the Soviet-American working summit in Reykjavík be described as totally unsuccessful? Of course not," says Radio Moscow. "After all, the exchange of opinions took place and, as Comrade Gorbachev has pointed out, this meeting has shown that the need for dialogue is even greater, although it must be very difficult." The Communist Party daily *Pravda* and the government newspaper *Izvestia*, for their part, claim that "ultra-right-wingers" like Republican congressman Jack Kemp of New York had pushed the president to cling to SDI. Finally, on the evening of October 13, Soviet television rebroadcast the press conference given by Mikhail Gorbachev the day before.

Beyond this press conference, how does Gorbachev emerge from the meeting in Reykjavík? One of his advisers, Anatoly Chernyaev, takes notes in the plane that carried the Soviet delegation from the Icelandic capital to Moscow on Sunday evening, October 12. The general secretary of the CPSU delivers a warm analysis of what has just happened. "The speculation began right away: who won over whom?" Chernyaev quotes

Gorbachev telling the delegation. "But that was not our goal when we went to Reykjavík. We had an important reason to take this initiative. The fact is that Geneva had ended in failure. We believed that a major breakthrough was necessary, because time plays against the interests of mankind."

Chernyaev continues in conclusion, "Finally, it was fairly easy to find an agreement on the first and second points of our platform—strategic weapons and intermediate-range missiles. . . . We understood the President's problems, that he was not free to make his own decisions. Thus, the Soviet leader interpreted Reagan's refusal as an inability to make a decision alone. Even though the prerogatives of the President of the United States, in the American Constitution, allow him to negotiate treaties, these must in turn, must be ratified by the Senate. We did not see as a tragedy that it was the SDI that prevented a Reykjavík success. We thought: let the President think about all this, take advice from Congress. Perhaps we will have to make further attempts to breach the barrier that still separates us. We can wait."

"We are not going to back out of our proposals in Reykjavík," Mikhail Gorbachev tells Chernyaev, adding that he had become "even more optimistic" since the end of the summit. For the Soviet leader, this meeting "is a step in a difficult and complicated dialogue, in search of solutions. These solutions must be large scale, justifying a global package and not a partial agreement."

The general secretary of the CPSU, in this debriefing with Chernyaev, then mentions two reasons why Westerners have false conceptions of the USSR. "The first is that the Russians would be afraid of SDI and therefore would be ready for all concessions. And the second that we would be more interested in disarmament than the Americans. These positions affected the discussions in Reykjavík. . . . Before, the conversation concerned only the limitation of nuclear weapons. Now it is about their reduction and elimination. From this point of view, we should avoid choosing paths which would lead to the superiority of one or the other. That is why joining the ABM Treaty has become a key issue. The US position on this issue made it clear that the United States had not abandoned any objective of superiority. That is why they have not had enough strength of character, responsibility, courage or political will to cross this threshold [of an agreement]. For this would have meant freeing themselves from their dependence on the military-industrial complex. With this package, we want to show the world—and in the first place Europeans—that SDI is the main obstacle to nuclear disarmament."

## Report to the Politburo

Unlike the American presidential system, with Ronald Reagan as the sole chief executive, Mikhail Gorbachev is not quite sole master of the Soviet ship. Instead, he must deal with the

Communist Party and the members of its governing body, the Politburo. On his return from Iceland, on Tuesday October 14, Gorbachev takes stock of its sixteen full members. Among those leaders of the USSR at the time were Andrei Gromyko, former minister of foreign affairs and president of the Supreme Soviet; Viktor Tchebrikov, head of the KGB; Anatoly Dobrynin, former Soviet ambassador to Washington; and Boris Yeltsin, who will play a key role in the ultimate collapse of the Soviet Union and Communism itself.

"Yesterday you all received the record of conversations with Reagan in Reykjavík," begins Gorbachev. "Today we must discuss the outcome of these negotiations and adopt a resolution. You have a draft of this resolution before you." The general secretary of the CPSU then summarizes the situation. The summit "has had a global echo. America is beginning to move, too. There are criticisms of Reagan. Some wonder if he did not choose to leave 'a bird in the bush rather than a bird in the hand.' Why have we failed to reach an agreement? This can be explained by a lot of objective and subjective factors. As far as Reagan was concerned, we had to battle in Reykjavík not only our leading enemy, but also a representative of our enemy who expressed many primitive, even caveman-like attitudes, and a certain intellectual incapacity. But this is not the main reason" for this failure to reach an agreement.

Gorbachev continues his introductory remarks for some time. He mentions two mistakes the Americans have made. "The first is tactical in nature. The Americans are convinced that we are demanding more than a disarmament agreement. They think that because of our internal difficulties, we should accept their proposals. They also misjudged my agreement on a visit to the United States. They thought I wanted to come at all costs because I needed to increase my political capital. Another mistake of a strategic nature is the idea that an arms race would exhaust us economically, create obstacles for Gorbachev and for the Soviet leadership as a whole, undermine our plans to resolve economic and social problems and thus cause popular discontent. Moreover, in this way they hope to limit the possibilities of economic ties between developing countries and the USSR and create a situation in which these countries would be forced to submit to the United States. Finally, their mistake is to believe that, with the help of SDI, they could undermine strategic parity and assert their military superiority. They do not know what our answer to SDI will be. All this determined their behavior in Reykjavík, their desire to limit discussions to a superficial level in order to silence the voices that oppose the policy of this administration. As can be seen now, this strategic line of the current administration is based on illusions."

After having established Reagan's errors of judgment, the general secretary turns to a description of his sense of the state of affairs post-Reykjavík. "A totally new situation has developed," he continues. "The discussion on nuclear disarmament has reached a new, higher level, if we are now to fight for the liquidation and a complete ban on nuclear weapons, to actively pursue our peaceful offensive. Ours is a strong position. It reflects a new thinking and is a practical application of the foreign policy goals that were highlighted by the XXVII Congress of the CPSU."

Then, satisfied, Gorbachev continues his argument. "The world considers that the failure of the agreement in Reykjavík is due to the United States. Cyrus Vance and other distinguished American political figures claim that Reykjavík is a defeat for the Republicans. The fact that we came to Reykjavík not with a list of disjointed proposals but with a package was of central importance. Since we had gone so far with our proposals, suggesting the total liquidation of nuclear weapons, we should have received total guarantees of our security. And only an agreement according to our conditions would have guaranteed that security. We will stand firm on that. Therefore, let us agree at the outset: we do not want some ministry of foreign affairs comments that contradict that. We do not need scattered morsels, just a complete 'package.'" He pauses a second. The whole of the Politburo approves in unison with a single word: "Perfect."

Now, Gorbachev continues. "After Reykjavík, we have accumulated more points than after Geneva. In a way, we changed places with the Americans. Before, we were generally behind them in promoting our vision of the world. We were late giving interviews, holding press conferences. This practice must develop now. Reykjavík must become a new beginning for our propaganda. By showing more aggressiveness, we should gain public support in foreign countries."

His report to the Politburo sheds an important light on Soviet defense strategy in the waning years of the Communist era. "This new situation post-Reykjavík requires a new approach in our military doctrine, in the building of our armed forces, in the defense industry. We need to think carefully about what needs to be done if there is to be no intermediate-range missile, what types of new weapons need to be developed. We need appropriate guidance on these issues. Our defense industry must match our military doctrine. We must not let pacifism penetrate our armed forces and our defense industry. It is important to ensure the inevitability of our second-strike potential. So we should not touch the defense budget. We should be particularly attentive to questions about our possible response to SDI."

Then Gorbachev concludes. "The meeting in Reykjavík revealed the representatives of the American administration as unscrupulous people, without any morals. Their line is pressure, deceit, or vicious mercantilism." There follows an instructive conversation between Gorbachev and the members of the Politburo.

Mikhail Zimyanin, editor-in-chief of the party daily *Pravda*, is the first to congratulate the Soviet leader. "You, Mikhail Sergeyevich, made a remarkable performance in the discussions and at the press conference."

"When I arrived at the press conference in Reykjavík, I noticed that the journalists were depressed," Gorbachev replies.

"I tried to dissolve the pessimism as much as I could. Of course, Reykjavík was far from leaving a joyful impression. When Reagan bade me farewell, he could not even look me in the eye."

Heydar Aliyev, longtime KGB general and leader of Azerbaijan, appointed by Andropov to the Politburo, now takes the floor. "I agree with Egor Kuzmitch [Ligachev], that Reykjavík gave us an advantage. The press conference held by Mikhail Sergeyevich was most effective. This snatched the mask from the face of the United States."

"You should remember," Gorbachev replies, "that we had in mind the following: either find an agreement in Reykjavík, or, in case of failure, use the summit to unmask American positions."

All the participants, without exception, praised Gorbachev's performance: "brilliant," "formidable," "remarkable negotiator." The Politburo is unanimous and feels that the Soviet Union has scored points not only against the Americans, but also in world opinion. No one at this meeting dares to criticize or to ask Gorbachev questions that are embarrassing or simply difficult. And he is now in a strong position of power at the peak of the Soviet system. Difficult to know if his Politburo comrades are really admiring him, or if they fear him. Perhaps a bit of both. But he has, quite simply, won his stripes.

While all members of the Politburo are calling on their propaganda to transform world opinion, Gromyko and Gorbachev engage in an interesting analysis of the disparate forces within the US delegation in Iceland.

"We must make our propaganda more active, in order to fully explain the novelty of our positions," Gromyko observes. "A real deluge of criticism fell on Reagan. Undoubtedly, this will be a severe defeat for the Republican party on the eve of the elections. And that also works to our advantage. Who supports Reagan? It is, above all, the arms makers."

"This was clear in Reykjavík," Gorbachev responds. "As soon as we started talking about serious things, Reagan told us he had to talk to the experts. And the experts who accompanied him to Reykjavík were mainly representatives of the right-wing reactionary forces. These reactionary political views are well known. But from a professional point of view, as [Marshal] Akhromeyev told me, they were well prepared."

"The forces that support Reagan are doing everything right now to influence American public opinion and polish the image of the administration in the wake of Reykjavík," Gromyko adds. "We should write more about SDI, to unmask it. There is a widely held view, for example, that SDI is a shield. What type of shield is it? Its objective is totally different" from what has been suggested so far.

## The End of a Tormented Year

In both camps, the post-Reykjavík posturing is complex. How to get the negotiations back on track, which have failed so close to a historic agreement? Of course, the discussions in Höfdi never progressed as far on nuclear disarmament as on other issues, including regional conflicts and human rights. But what are the next steps to continue the process initiated in Geneva in 1985? No state visits are planned between the two leaders. For the moment, then, dialogue must resume at lower levels.

Between mid-October and December 1986, Soviet leaders sought to continue the battle for hearts and minds—a contest they believe they won in Iceland, in a certain way. Gorbachev succeeded in presenting the Americans as the ones who had torpedoed the prospects for a historic agreement.

Behind the scenes, the Soviet leader tries to press his advantage. In a series of meetings with the Politburo, he continues to explain his strategy. "What does America want? They manipulate, revise Reykjavík, move away from it," he points out. "They have returned to provocations, ending the good climate of our relations. . . . We are at a difficult stage. We must respond strongly, but must not go so far as to cause an acceleration of the arms race. The results of Reykjavík, despite the absence of agreements, exceeded expectations. And now the Americans are starting to distance themselves from these gains. Reykjavík was a success in the peace process. It frightened the Americans and they returned to their hard line. They do this because they cannot change the process we initiated."

But Chernyaev, in his chronicle of these Politburo meetings, does not hesitate to criticize Gorbachev. "On the central theme—the arms race—Gorbachev did not flinch," he writes.

"But even in this area, he did not see the problem in all its complexities. For example, a real breakthrough in building Western confidence in us would have been to extend our moratorium on nuclear testing. But no! Gorbachev yielded to the pressure of our military-industrial complex and the argument that [our forces] might be outdated."

Chernyaev has not finished settling his accounts with the general secretary. He is very critical of Gorbachev's handling of the war in Afghanistan, but above all describes Gorbachev as ready to abandon some of his ideas in the face of the pressure exerted by soldiers of the Red Army. "Gorbachev has been seized by the concept of parity between the two superpowers and other aspects of the old foreign policy thinking contained in the top-secret reports of agencies linked to the military-industrial complex. He let himself be convinced that we had 'an answer to SDI' and that it would be a surprise to [the Americans]. I tried to provide him with a different perspective, particularly from astronaut Vladimir Aksionov, who was involved in this field and brought me data and analysis showing that our own SDI project was just throwing money out the window. But these attempts on my part were met with an immediate refusal: 'You don't know anything about it, stay out of it!' In this connection, it is interesting to note that several Soviet reports refer to a Russian SDI that would not have succeeded."

On November 27, Gorbachev is in India. With Prime Minister Rajiv Gandhi, he signs the Delhi Declaration. "In the nuclear age, humanity must develop new political thinking, a new world view, to guarantee the survival of humanity," the declaration reads. "We have inherited a world that belongs not only to the present generation, but to future generations, and it requires priority for universal human values." After this preamble, the declaration goes on to observe that "the balance of terror" must be replaced by a "global system of international security."

## Defeat in the Midterms

Washington is trying to regain control. The midterm elections are held on November 4. As expected, the Democrats retain a majority in the House of Representatives, even gaining five seats (258 Democratic seats against 177 Republican seats). Worse for the Reagan administration, Republicans also lose their majority in the Senate, with Democrats winning eight seats, and thus a comfortable margin of fifty-five to forty-five. Americans voters have demonstrated their disaffection with the White House tenant, who finds himself isolated and, at least in a legislative sense, powerless for the last two years of his term and of his presidency.

Around the president, there is intense debate over how to proceed. In January 1987, a number of notes land on Reagan's desk—all with the goal of reviving the Geneva process. One such report by the National Intelligence Council entitled "Soviet and Foreign Reactions to a world with Zero Ballistic Missiles" observes that the election results demonstrate that Americans do not trust the Soviets—and perhaps even less after Reykjavík. "There are strong and compelling reasons—doctrinal, institutional, bureaucratic, personal, economic and strategic—for the USSR to reject proposals that promise to eradicate the arsenal of ballistic missiles of the USSR."

The document, even today still partly classified as top secret, warns that the situation could get worse. "While it is unclear, in a zero-ballistic missile world, if the risk of escalating from a conventional war to a nuclear war will decrease, the likelihood of crises and even conventional conflicts, could increase." The authors of the report, which is probably a synthesis of the analyses from various American intelligence agencies, try to foresee the Soviets' intentions. "Achieving Gorbachev's two main objectives on arms control—stopping SDI and diverting the Reagan administration from its comprehensive national security agenda of rearmament and anti-Soviet actions—would make the 1990s much easier for the USSR. [These objectives] would reconcile Soviet economic and social modernization with the continuation, or even increase, of its role as an international superpower." Of course the report was based on the all-but-universal belief that Soviet Communism would exist throughout the next decade. Indeed, it was barely two years from extinction.

This worst-case scenario spans forty pages. And it reflects another fear in the White House: how to maintain deterrence of nuclear war if America considerably reduces its nuclear arsenal? In a memorandum dated January 5, 1987, William Cockell, a former Navy admiral on Reagan's National Security Council staff, summarizes a meeting between Reagan, the Joint Chiefs of Staff and other officials of the State and Defense Departments. The central question at issue: Is it possible to maintain a credible deterrence with strategic forces that would be reduced by 50 percent in five years; or if ballistic missiles are eliminated entirely? The answer: The chiefs of staff are reasonably comfortable with the 50 percent goal of five years. But not the zero goal of ten years. The meeting follows a presidential directive requesting the joint chiefs to study the application of total elimination of strategic nuclear weapons. In other words, Ronald Reagan, in mid-December 1986, asks his teams to study the application of the principles discussed in Reykjavík.

At the same time, the Department of State is working in the same direction, reflecting on what might have happened if an agreement been reached in Iceland. Secretary of State George Shultz delivers a speech at the University of Chicago on November 17, 1986, on "Nuclear Weapons, Arms Control and the Future of Deterrence," asserting that the US delegation in Geneva was ready to pick up negotiations where the debates in Reykjavík had ended.

"All this is part of a full and complete program for all of us," Shultz assures his audience. Ambitious? Yes. Unrealistic? No. "I think that on the basis of the progress made in

Reykjavík, substantial reductions in Soviet and American nuclear weapons are possible, and that can be done in stages and in a stable way. But we have to think a lot about how to proceed. It is a difficult task as we seek to create conditions that would ensure the security and freedom of our country and our allies without the constant threat of a nuclear disaster."

At the White House, the Pentagon, and the State Department, the next steps are being prepared. In a series of notes intended for Ronald Reagan, the argument is being made that the administration must at all costs detach itself from Reykjavík. In a document "US-Soviet Relations: Where Do We Go from Here?" John Poindexter analyzes both Soviet attitudes and American strategy of the future, then lists five steps to follow. Secretary of State George Shultz sends his own recommendations. Among them, "get away from the word laboratory that has done so much damage to the presidency." This is followed by "Instructions for the Geneva Negotiators" from the Department of Defense, with heavy input from Richard Perle, which insists on "not allowing the Soviets to negotiate additional limits on SDI." Finally, on October 16, Poindexter sends a six-page brief to the president on the theme: "Why we cannot commit ourselves to eliminate all nuclear weapons in ten years." That is exactly the opposite of what had been discussed a few days earlier in Iceland. The Reagan administration risks finding itself in complete self-contradiction.

In the end, the Reykjavík Summit will not have been a total failure. The two leaders meet twice again—in Washington from December 7 to 10, 1987, where they sign an Intermediate-Range Nuclear Forces Treaty (INF) Treaty, and again from May 29 to June 1, 1988, when it's Ronald Reagan's turn to go to Moscow for the leaders' fourth summit. On December 7, 1988, a final meeting is held in New York in the presence of President-elect George H. W. Bush. However, Mikhail Gorbachev is forced to cut the meeting short to return to the USSR following a devastating earthquake in Armenia. It is only a year later, on December 2 and 3, 1989, right after the Berlin Wall falls, that Bush and Gorbachev meet in Malta. Until the final collapse of the Soviet Union in December 1991, the two leaders see each other six more times, either at bilateral summits or on the sidelines of international meetings. On July 31, 1991, in Moscow, Bush and Gorbachev finally sign the first nuclear disarmament treaty between the two powers—the first direct consequence of the Reykjavík Summit. This is START I (Strategic Arms Reduction Treaty). It comes into force on December 5, 1994, and expires fifteen years later on December 5, 2009.

"Under START I, the Soviet Union and the United States are required to reduce the number of their strategic nuclear warheads to 6,000 units each. These warheads can be attributed to up to 1,600 strategic missiles or heavy bombers," the UN Disarmament Affairs Office says. "These reductions in the number of nuclear warheads and vectors [delivery devices] must be applied in three phases over a period of seven years after the entry into force of the treaty [i.e. before December 2001]. Existing equipment may be upgraded and replaced, but the Parties undertake not to manufacture, test in flight or deploy modified or new types of intercontinental ballistic missiles (ICBM) or submarine-launched ballistic missiles (SLBM) with more than ten warheads. . . . The number of warheads assigned to a missile shall not be reduced by more than four and the number of warheads so removed shall not exceed 1,250."

The disintegration of the Soviet Union at the end of 1991, however, complicates the implementation of START. On May 23, 1992, the Lisbon Protocol to the treaty recognizes that the Russian Federation, Belarus, Kazakhstan, and Ukraine have become the legal successors of the Soviet Union. In this text, Belarus, Ukraine, and Kazakhstan "undertake to eliminate all nuclear weapons within their territory and to accede to the non-proliferation treaty as non-nuclear-weapon States." Thus, START itself is ratified by Russia and the United States.

## Was the SDI Project Viable?

An irony of history. The Reykjavík Summit says a lot about ideologies during the Cold War; about the cultural differences between Russians and Americans; about the psychological dimension of two world leaders, each of whom seeks to tame the other. On the unspoken words of two declared enemies who try to break through the secrets in each case so closely guarded by the other. But the ultimate irony is that in the wake of these meetings in 1986, history does not have the last word. Only time now allows us to know that the psychodrama in Iceland was based on ephemerals as intangible as the winds that swept the Icelandic coast.

SDI, so dear to Reagan, could never have been achieved within the expected ten years.

In the opinion of Joseph Schwartz, one of the pioneers of laser technology, "at least twenty years would have been necessary to develop something operational." This Israeli-American, a product of Massachusetts Institute of Technology (MIT), participated in the earliest developments of laser technology in the 1960s and 1970s, the time of the first major technical breakthroughs in laser theory and practice. Schwartz observes that when Ronald Reagan mentioned the SDI project for the first time in 1983, almost no scientist believed in the feasibility of the project.

"There was a gap between having a power source and building a power system which can be used in space. There was certainly potential, but many projects had been studied and then abandoned."

In the most basic terms, the idea of launching and placing in orbit satellites equipped with laser beams capable of destroying missiles in full flight—which has been likened to shooting a bullet with a bullet—was simply not feasible. If an SDI concept worked "on paper," the application of such a system could not have been implemented within the ten years that Gorbachev raised in Reykjavík. Today, thirty years later, it is still not functional. Indeed, the first workable antimissile defense system is a land-based system that launches an antimissile missile to serve as an interceptor—and that only in 2017.

"At that time, late 1970s or early 1980s, the most advanced lasers were chemical lasers. In order to compress the light, the molecules are excited by a chemical mixture heated by gasoline and oxidizing liquids. They burn together in a combustion chamber and at that point a powerful laser can be created," Schwartz explains. We must therefore imagine a very large, very heavy satellite launched in space and placed in orbit. "To produce a laser with a power of 700 kilowatts, which is the perfect threshold for a destructive laser beam—and this power was achieved in the laboratory in 1984—it takes a lot of space. Imagine something the size of a building. At the time, these lasers were tested in huge laboratories and there were not many real efforts to miniaturize them. So it was effectively impossible to send such a device into space. Especially in multiple copies. Not to mention maintenance or repair in case of problems," although, Schwartz concedes, "the repair system could have been included in the equipment and triggered remotely." If the problem was critical, Schwartz observes, it would have been possible to send an astronaut to deal with it. But it would have been even more complex than the Hubble Space Telescope because of the chemical engine. And once the fuel was consumed by laser shots, it would be necessary to refuel them.

Nevertheless, at the time Americans, Israelis, and others were also working on lasers generated by sunlight rather than by chemical heating. "Between 1984 and 1987, at the Weizmann Institute of Science in Israel, I worked on lasers fueled by the sun," Schwartz continues. "It was another method, which was never developed on any large scale. It was all about recovering and converting sunlight. But to use it in space, solar radiation is too diffuse and too low energy."

Beyond the all-but-insurmountable technical barriers, Schwarz mentions the financial aspects—dozens of satellites armed with lasers. "It was too big, too complex and too expensive," Schwartz concludes. At least one billion dollars was spent by the Pentagon over a decade starting in the 1980s. US companies in the aeronautics, aerospace, and armaments industries profited enormously from these SDI projects, all eventually abandoned by 1996. "Under the Clinton presidency," says Schwartz, "the idea of missile defense was in the theater of operations, a ground-based defense system. So we are far from Star Wars."

While the Reagan administration was so intent on launching its ill-fated SDI project, what was going on in Moscow? "We knew this was not feasible in ten years," Pavel Palazchenko says today. "On the other hand, there was the official position that this project was very dangerous. The Soviet Union had asked for an agreement that these space stations would never target the Earth. I heard our specialists, like Sagdeev, say it was not feasible. The priority of the Gorbachev team was to ensure that there is an organic link between a missile defense system and offensive missiles, and that this should be included in all treaties. This is the position that Russia is taking now, and I think that is the right one. . . . According to American articles published then, however, some systems could have been deployed in space, even just for show. But this would have had a devastating effect on the ongoing negotiations."

On the Soviet side, Gorbachev continued to place his full trust in his experts, including Roald Sagdeev, who told him: "According to the laws of physics, this is not something that can be done in the near future." That being so, and since nothing is simple in international relations, at least two sources have recently revealed that the Soviets were also launching their own Star Wars project. Sagdeev, director of the Moscow Space Academy and Gorbachev's nuclear adviser, of course knew that the military had been discussing such a concept as early as the 1970s. This is confirmed by Palazchenko: "Yes, there was a project in the early stages of development, an anti-satellite project. I think there had been some tests. Not in the laboratory, but in space. Something was launched. There were two or three people who promoted this project, which could be turned into an anti-missile program."

This former diplomat and interpreter, who has remained close to Gorbachev until today, goes even further in detailing what he knows about the nature and extent of such projects. "The spirit of this research is purely technical. If we say, 'Let's go to Mars,' they'll press full speed ahead. But they don't think in financial terms. In the 1970s, however, the Soviet Union could no longer afford a space race with the Americans. So we should not take too seriously those people who wanted to do this type of project. I do not think it was very realistic. Gorbachev respected the advice of the Academy of Sciences, whose leaders said, 'Let's not go in that direction.' It's as simple as that."

So, neither the American Star Wars nor its Soviet equivalent— if indeed there ever was one—was successful.

# NINE

## *A World Without Nuclear Bombs*

Reagan and Gorbachev; Bush and Gorbachev; Clinton and Yeltsin; Bush and Putin; Obama and Medvedev; Obama and Putin; Trump and Putin.

The pairs follow one after the other, without really resembling each other. But the central issue of nuclear disarmament has remained for all these years. More than three decades separate us from the Reykjavík Summit. A historic opportunity missed, although somewhat overtaken by other world events. The dialogue never stopped between the two great powers, even after the break-up of the Soviet Union in December 1991 and the creation of the Russian Federation. Eventually, after the SALT I and II treaties in the 1970s, and then START in 1988, the United States and Russia signed three additional nuclear arms reduction treaties.

## A Fourth START Treaty

Today, START 4 is in force. Nicknamed "New START," it was signed on April 8, 2010, by Barack Obama and Dmitry Medvedev, then president of Russia, in Prague, capital of the Czech Republic, and is being applied after ratification by the legislatures of both countries. By January 2015, seventeen compliance verification visits had been conducted on each side.

What does the treaty provide? The two powers must limit their number of nuclear warheads to 1,550. This is 74 percent less than the START I treaty signed in 1991. The text specifies that all nuclear warheads must be able to be launched by submarines, by bombers, or from land bases. The treaty also limits the numbers of missiles themselves to 700 units for those already deployed, and to 800 for those not yet deployed.

## A Dream Come True

For the last American president the halo of the Nobel Peace Prize, awarded in his first year as president in 2009, also invokes the aura of a world without nuclear weapons. It is in Prague on April 5, 2009, when Obama, in office barely two-and-a-half months, delivers an open-air speech on Hradschin Square, in front of the castle overlooking the city, and reaffirms Reagan's dream. In the presence of the Czech president and prime minister, before a crowd estimated at thirty thousand people, the president of the United States pays tribute to the heroes of the Velvet Revolution who paved the way for a peaceful transition to democracy at the end of 1989. Early in his address, Barack Obama addresses the issue of nuclear weapons.

"One of those issues that I'll focus on today is fundamental to the security of our nations and to the peace of the world—that's the future of nuclear weapons in the 21st century," he says. "The existence of thousands of nuclear weapons is the most dangerous legacy of the Cold War. No nuclear war was fought between the United States and the Soviet Union, but generations lived with the knowledge that their world could be erased in a single flash of light. Cities like Prague that had existed for centuries, that embodied the beauty and the talent of so much of humanity, would have ceased to exist. Today, the Cold War has disappeared but thousands of those weapons have not. In a strange turn of history, the threat of global nuclear war has gone down, but the risk of a nuclear attack has gone up. More nations have acquired these weapons. Testing has continued. Black market trade in nuclear secrets and nuclear materials abound. The technology to build a bomb has spread. Terrorists are determined to buy, build or steal one. Our efforts to contain these dangers are centered on a global non-proliferation regime, but as more people and nations break the rules, we could reach the point where the center cannot hold."

The statement is clear. The point is strong, if tinged with pacifism—Barack Obama was determined to remain faithful to his presidential campaign, which was based on hope. But Obama also takes his responsibilities seriously as the leader of a great nuclear power. "Some argue that the spread of these weapons cannot be stopped, cannot be checked—that we are destined to live in a world where more nations and more people possess the ultimate tools of destruction. Such fatalism is a deadly adversary, for if we believe that the spread of nuclear weapons is inevitable, then in some way we are admitting to ourselves that the use of nuclear weapons is inevitable. Just as we stood for freedom in the 20th century, we must stand together for the right of people everywhere to live free from fear in the 21st century." The crowd applauds. "As a nuclear power, as the only nuclear power to have used a nuclear weapon, the United States has a moral responsibility to act. We cannot succeed in this endeavor alone, but we can lead it, we can start it."

Then comes the heart of the announcement, which will help earn him the Nobel Prize: "So today, I state clearly and with conviction America's commitment to seek the peace and security of a world without nuclear weapons." There is more applause. "This goal will not be reached quickly—perhaps not in my lifetime. It will take patience and persistence. But now we, too, must ignore the voices who tell us that the world cannot change. We have to insist, 'Yes, we can.'" A reference, met too with applause, to his campaign slogan for the presidency.

But now, the American president is going to issue a challenge: "To put an end to Cold War thinking, we will reduce the role of nuclear weapons in our national security strategy, and urge others to do the same. Make no mistake: As long as these weapons exist, the United States will maintain a safe, secure and effective arsenal to deter any adversary, and guarantee that defense to our allies—including the Czech Republic. But we will begin the work of reducing our arsenal."

A president of the United States has now publicly called, again, for the elimination of nuclear weapons in the world. The message is strong. But he immediately states that the United States will, in the interim, retain a large arsenal of nuclear deterrence.

The distant successor to Ronald Reagan in the White House details his plan in several stages. The first is for the Senate to ratify the Nuclear Test Ban Treaty and negotiate a new international treaty to stop the spread of fissile materials for military purposes. Second, the Nuclear Non-Proliferation Treaty should be strengthened.

The contract is simple, he says: "Countries with nuclear weapons will move towards disarmament, countries without nuclear weapons will not acquire them, and all countries can access peaceful nuclear energy. . . . We need more resources and authority to strengthen international inspections." Obama also proposes the creation of an international nuclear "fuel bank," which all signatories of the nonproliferation treaty can have access to.

Still, he is not unaware of the risks. "We need real and immediate consequences for countries caught breaking the rules or trying to leave the treaty without cause." He refers explicitly to North Korea, which is acknowledged to have produced nuclear weapons; and Iran, which has said it does not seek to obtain the bomb, but is reluctant to comply with the multinational mandates of the International Atomic Energy Agency. Obama closes his speech with a pledge to embark on a "new international effort to secure all vulnerable nuclear material around the world within four years" with the implication that they should not fall into the hands of terrorists.

## Summits on "Nuclear Security"

The American president takes the lead in organizing the first International Summit on Nuclear Security in Washington, DC, on April 12–13, 2010, one year after his speech in Prague.

Leaders of most of the world's large and medium-sized powers gather for this occasion, particularly representatives of the countries holding nuclear weapons: Barack Obama (United States), Dmitry Medvedev (Russia), David Miliband

(United Kingdom, minister of foreign affairs), Nicolas Sarkozy (France), Hu Jintao (China), Dan Meridor (Israel, deputy prime minister, though Israel has never acknowledged possession of a nuclear weapon), Manmohan Singh (India), and Youssouf Raza Gilani (Pakistan). The secretary-general of the United Nations Ban Ki Moon is there, as well as the director general of the International Atomic Energy Agency (IAEA), Yukiya Amano of Japan. Finally, other influential countries have sent representatives, including the prime minister of Japan Yukio Hatoyama, the only victim of an atomic attack at the summit, as well as representatives from Germany, Brazil, Canada, Saudi Arabia, and South Africa. Former members of the USSR or the Eastern Europe Communist bloc—Ukraine, the Czech Republic, Poland, Georgia, and Kazakhstan—also send representatives. Unsurprisingly, neither Iran nor North Korea are present, though the international community has evidence to suggest that both countries are building or already possess a nuclear arsenal.

For two days, this unprecedented gathering of world leaders addresses the issue of nuclear weapons at the highest levels at the Walter E. Washington Convention Center, barely a dozen blocks from the White House. An ambitious official statement emerges—though as is often the case at this type of international summit, the communiqué should be viewed with some skepticism. However, with the attention of the world press, it is clearly a success—especially for Barack Obama.

The concluding document encompasses a prelude and twelve central points:

>Nuclear terrorism is one of the most challenging threats to international security, and strong nuclear security measures are the most effective means to prevent terrorists, criminals, or other unauthorized actors from acquiring nuclear materials. In addition to our shared goals of nuclear disarmament, nuclear nonproliferation and peaceful uses of nuclear energy, we also all share the objective of nuclear security. Therefore, those gathered here in Washington, D.C., on April 13, 2010, commit to strengthen nuclear security and reduce the threat of nuclear terrorism. Success will require responsible national actions and sustained and effective international cooperation.

>We welcome and join President Obama's call to secure all vulnerable nuclear material in four years, as we work together to enhance nuclear security. Therefore, we:

>1   Reaffirm the fundamental responsibility of States, consistent with their respective international obligations, to maintain effective security of all nuclear materials, which

includes nuclear materials used in nuclear weapons, and nuclear facilities under their control; to prevent non-state actors from obtaining the information or technology required to use such material for malicious purposes; and emphasize the importance of robust national legislative and regulatory frameworks for nuclear security;

2   Call on States to work cooperatively as an international community to advance nuclear security, requesting and providing assistance as necessary;

3   Recognize that highly enriched uranium and separated plutonium require special precautions and agree to promote measures to secure, account for, and consolidate these materials, as appropriate; and encourage the conversion of reactors from highly enriched to low enriched uranium fuel and minimization of use of highly enriched uranium, where technically and economically feasible;

4   Endeavor to fully implement all existing nuclear security commitments and work toward acceding to those not yet joined, consistent with national laws, policies and procedures;

5   Support the objectives of international nuclear security instruments, including the Convention on the Physical Protection of Nuclear Material, as amended, and the International Convention for the Suppression of Acts of Nuclear Terrorism, as essential elements of the global nuclear security architecture;

6   Reaffirm the essential role of the International Atomic Energy Agency in the international nuclear security framework and will work to ensure that it continues to have the appropriate structure, resources and expertise needed to carry out its mandated nuclear security activities in accordance with its Statute, relevant General Conference resolutions and its Nuclear Security Plans;

7   Recognize the role and contributions of the United Nations as well as the contributions of the Global Initiative to Combat Nuclear Terrorism and the G-8-led Global Partnership Against the Spread of Weapons and Materials of Mass Destruction within their respective mandates and memberships;

8   Acknowledge the need for capacity building for nuclear security and cooperation at bilateral, regional and multilateral levels for the

promotion of nuclear security culture through technology development, human resource development, education, and training; and stress the importance of optimizing international cooperation and coordination of assistance;

9    Recognize the need for cooperation among States to effectively prevent and respond to incidents of illicit nuclear trafficking; and agree to share, subject to respective national laws and procedures, information and expertise through bilateral and multilateral mechanisms in relevant areas such as nuclear detection, forensics, law enforcement, and the development of new technologies;

10   Recognize the continuing role of nuclear industry, including the private sector, in nuclear security and will work with industry to ensure the necessary priority of physical protection, material accountancy, and security culture;

11   Support the implementation of strong nuclear security practices that will not infringe upon the rights of States to develop and utilize nuclear energy for peaceful purposes and technology and will facilitate international cooperation in the field of nuclear security; and

12  Recognize that measures contributing to nuclear material security have value in relation to the security of radioactive substances and encourage efforts to secure those materials as well.

Maintaining effective nuclear security will require continuous national efforts facilitated by international cooperation and undertaken on a voluntary basis by States. We will promote the strengthening of global nuclear security through dialogue and cooperation with all states. Thus, we issue the Work Plan as guidance for national and international action including through cooperation within the context of relevant international forums and organizations.

Afterwards, three other international summits on nuclear security would be held—in March 2012 in Seoul, March 2014 in The Hague, and March and April 2016, again in Washington.

## Hacking and Acts of Terrorism

An act of nuclear terrorism is the greatest fear of the international community. This fear is not a new one, but it became a clear and present danger in the wake of the September 11,

2001, attack on the United States. Security and defense policy specialist Graham Allison has posited that the world is only barely managing to avoid a catastrophe every day. Former assistant secretary of defense for Bill Clinton's first term (1993–1997), and now a professor at Harvard University's Kennedy School, Allison details in a book published in 2004 called *Nuclear Terrorism: The Ultimate Preventable Catastrophe*, the risks of a nuclear device falling into the hands of al-Qaeda or another jihadi group.

"I say precisely this: if nations like the United States, Russia, Pakistan, France do not now take matters in hand, I believe we will soon see a nuclear September 11. Someone will blow up an atomic bomb in a large city, American, Russian or European. And when this happens once, there is no reason to think that it will not happen again," he warns. He bases his argument on several specific cases. "We know that al-Qaeda has been trying to get an atomic bomb for more than ten years, that they have been led to believe two or three times that they were buying nuclear material. Thus, two Pakistani scientists who had worked on the atomic bomb in their country met bin Laden in Afghanistan. He showed them the uranium he had bought in Uzbekistan and they had to explain to him that this uranium was not enriched enough to make a bomb."

According to Allison, as of 2004 there was at least one substantial alert in the United States after September 11—the "Dragonfire" case. "One year to the day after September 11,

2001, George Tenet, then director of the CIA, entered the Oval Office for the president's daily briefing on intelligence matters. He told George W. Bush that according to a CIA agent, codenamed Dragonfire, al-Qaeda had acquired a small atomic bomb from a former USSR arsenal. And that bomb was somewhere in New York. Once those at the briefing had caught their breath, there followed a series of questions: did the Russian agent understand the type of bomb described by Dragonfire? Yes. Would Moscow guarantee 100 percent of all its weapons? Not sure. Did al-Qaeda carry the bomb to New York without anyone knowing? Yes.

"There was no solid basis for not taking Dragonfire seriously. The procedure established during the Cold War, called 'continuity of government' was immediately invoked. To prevent the country from being decapitated in the event of an attack—for the bomb could also be in Washington—Vice President Dick Cheney was evacuated to a secret site, accompanied by hundreds of officials, for several weeks. Nuclear scientists, engineers and physicists, were sent to New York to search for signs of radioactivity, although the chances of finding such traces were slim because such a weapon emitted little external radiation until detonated. Rudolph Giuliani, who at the time was the mayor of New York, was not informed. A leak to the press, with the still sensitive context of September 11, would have created a substantial panic. At the end of the day, the Dragonfire affair turned out to be a false alarm. But what is important in the story is that no one had the means to invalidate this information. It was taken seriously because it was probable."

Graham Allison identifies the key question—how likely is such a scenario? The thousands of nuclear warheads inherited from the entire USSR could not all be secured at the time of the collapse of the Soviet empire. Pakistan, a nuclear power, is also a cause for concern, both because of the internal struggles within its army and its support for the Taliban. Pakistan's conflict with India in Kashmir is also one of the most explosive on the planet. Finally, the questions of Iran and North Korea are still far from being resolved.

## The Danger of the Accident

Eric Schlosser, an American journalist and writer, has also sounded an alarm. His 2013 best seller, *Command and Control: Nuclear Weapons, the Damascus Accident and the Illusion of Safety*, lists all the nuclear incidents that have occurred on American territory from the Cold War to the present day. The least that can be said is that a nuclear explosion has been only a heartbeat away on innumerable occasions. He reports, minute by minute, an incident on a US nuclear base in 1980. "This incident was the subject of a congressional report that had been totally forgotten," he wrote. "The congressman representing the district, before his death, donated a copy of this report to the local university library, which I was able to consult."

The incident took place in Damascus, Arkansas, near Little Rock. On a US Air Force base, there was a Titan II missile armed with a nuclear warhead "equivalent to three times the power of all bombs dropped during the Second World War, including the two atomic bombs," writes Eric Schlosser. The missile nearly exploded. The accident took place on the night of September 18 to 19. It all started shortly after 6 P.M. "Two workers were involved in maintenance in the silo of the missile," says Schlosser. "It was routine, something they did every day. One of them had to unscrew a plate and when he took out his tool, the case fell, bouncing off the platform. He stretched out his hand to catch it, and missed it. The case fell into the tiny space between the platform and the missile. It fell about 60 feet, bounced off the silo, and ricocheted onto the missile, puncturing its skin. And suddenly, thousands of gallons of highly explosive and toxic rocket fuel began to fill the silo. The Air Force had no idea what to do. This missile had been on constant alert for seventeen years. These maintenance routines were practiced every day, but suddenly they were confronted with a situation they had never considered before."

The inevitable happened. Around three o'clock in the morning, the fuel exploded. Fortunately, the base had been almost completely evacuated. But the nuclear warhead, placed atop the Titan II, was propelled about 100 feet from its location on the ground near the entrance to the launch site. Fortunately, the security systems worked and it did not explode.

No radioactive leakage occurred. In the end, the accident of Damascus left one person dead and several wounded.

Eric Schlosser does not stop there, since the list of aberrant and dangerous situations is long. For ten years, during the Cold War, the US government maintained a B-52 bomber constantly in flight, armed with four hydrogen bombs. In the event of a Soviet attack and destruction of the entire American arsenal, these "flying weapons" would be all that was left to respond. During these long rotations, the crew was provided with rubber cushions, for better comfort. After a time, a strong smell flooded the cabin. One of the cushions, placed near the heater, had caught fire. The pilot requested permission to make an emergency landing at a top-secret air force base, unknown to the general public, in Greenland. The B-52, by then engulfed in flames, crashed a few feet from the airstrip. Another miracle: none of the four nuclear bombs exploded.

Back to 1980: President Jimmy Carter's national security adviser, Zbigniew Brzezinski, is sleeping peacefully next to his wife in Washington when his phone wakes him up. At the other end of the line is General William Odom, his military aide. "He tells him that 220 Soviet missiles have been launched and are headed for Washington," writes Eric Schlosser. Brzezinski asks Odom to confirm and call him back. The phone rings again in a few minutes. General Odom says: "It's a mistake, two thousand two hundred and twenty missiles are set to arrive." Brzezinski decides not to wake his wife. Washington will be wiped off the map within a few minutes. It's better that she dies in her sleep. He is about to call President Jimmy Carter to discuss the response when the phone rings again. "False alarm," Odom tells Brzezinski.

Ultimately, it was a chip problem. The computers used by NORAD, the US North American Air Defense command, "were already obsolete when they were installed in all bases in the early 1970s," said Schlosser. And there were other incidents of this kind, false alarms about missiles supposedly launched by Moscow. This raises a central question about computing. Today, security around US nuclear weapons is not ideal. The computer system that allows the transmission of the firing orders from top to bottom—from the president of the United States to the operators who launch the missile, whether from a land base, submarine, or bomber aircraft, is very old. Can the transmitted code be intercepted by an enemy? Pirated by a terrorist group? The question deserves to be asked and troubles many specialists.

In a recent report on the CBS news program *60 Minutes*, missile control was shown still to be using 5.25 inch floppy disks, a technology that appeared in 1976 and was already obsolete with the arrival of the first hard disks in 1981. Queried by journalist Lesley Stahl, Major General Jack Weinstein, commander of the US Air Force missile corps, said the diskettes were "extremely safe" and would escape hackers, since they were not connected to the Internet. In the same report, taped at F. E. Warren Air Force Base in Cheyenne, Wyoming, we can see old analog phones, kept online for the same concern—to avoid piracy.

## A Dangerously Aging Arsenal

In the United States, the obsolescence of the nuclear arsenal is repeatedly highlighted in the press. The *Los Angeles Times*, the fourth largest US daily newspaper, reports that "a number of military strategists, scientists and congressional leaders are calling for a new generation of hydrogen bombs." The *Times* explains that "nuclear warheads in the nation's arsenal average twenty-seven years old, which causes serious concerns about their security." John Hamre, deputy secretary of defense in the Clinton administration, now president of the Center for Strategic and International Studies, expressed his belief to the *Los Angeles Times* that "we should get rid of our existing warheads and develop new ones that we would test. We have the worst of all of situations: we stockpile old obsolete weapons in large quantities, which we keep because we fear they are no longer reliable." In the same newspaper survey, the chairman of the House Armed Services Committee, the Texas congressman Mac Thornberry, adds that "this is common sense. If you want to keep a machine alive well after its expiry date, you are walking on eggs. Not to mention that we are always spending more to stay in this situation."

For his part, John Foster, a former chief of research at the Pentagon during the Cold War and former director of the Lawrence Livermore National Laboratory, says that "two decades after the end of the Cold War, our nuclear deterrence could be in a much worse state than we think." Indeed, President George W. Bush had already halved the stock of nuclear warheads between 2001 and 2009.

## A Revival of Nuclear Spending

In order to modernize its nuclear arsenal, the United States has chosen to invest no less than $60 billion. More precisely, it is a question of modernizing the whole atomic energy complex as well as the nuclear weapons stockpile. At the heart of this project is a new form of controversial bomb, the interoperable nuclear warhead. Nicknamed the "Frankenbomb" by its opponents, this warhead would be composed of several parts, each with a different origin. "Mixing pieces in configurations that have never been tested cannot be a good idea," says Kingston Reif, director of disarmament and threat reduction policy at the Arms Control Association. "This is going to cost money that we do not have for a mission [nuclear deterrence] that is playing an increasingly limited role in the national security of the United States."

At the same time, the United States is increasing the production of fissionable nuclear material at a pace not seen since the end of the Cold War. According to the *Los Angeles Times*, the Department of Energy plans to produce eighty plutonium cores per year until 2030. During the decade from 2015 to 2025, the federal government plans to spend $355 billion to modernize the nation's nuclear arsenal, though there were already 15,000 weapons in reserve in a Texas warehouse.

"I see no justification for producing fifty to eighty warheads per year until 2030," says James Doyle, a former scientist with the Nuclear Non-Proliferation Division of the Los Alamos National Laboratory, when he called publicly for nuclear disarmament in 2014.

## A World without Weapons

In fact, several policy-makers, American and otherwise, have recently spoken in favor of a total revision of the most fundamental principles of nuclear deterrence. Senator Dianne Feinstein has gone the furthest in this respect. This California Democrat, a member of the Senate Intelligence Committee, in a column in the *Washington Post* in 2014, questioned the need for a vast nuclear arsenal any more. "Today, nuclear weapons are seen as a financial burden and a threat to global security," she said, coming straight to the central point. "Furthermore, our nuclear stockpile is competing for limited defense spending, money that could be used to address more pressing challenges such as the fight against the Islamic State and defending against cyberattacks.

GUILLAUME SERINA

"The United States currently maintains 4,804 nuclear weapons. If you include retired weapons that are awaiting dismantlement and the thousands of components in storage, the United States has the equivalent of around 10,000 weapons. When you consider that the weapons we maintain today are up to 100 times more destructive than the ones used in Hiroshima and Nagasaki, it becomes clear that the only value they offer is in deterring a nuclear attack.

"Over the past five years, the U.S. stockpile has been reduced by only 309 warheads, the slowest five-year reduction in more than two decades. More worrisome is the staggering cost of these weapons. In just the past three years, the budget for simply maintaining nuclear warheads and production facilities has grown from $6.9 billion to $8 billion a year, almost a 16 percent increase. In an era of budget 'sequestration,' when we're supposed to cut the defense budget by about $29 billion per year, our nuclear modernization plans are taking us in the opposite direction. . . . Put simply, the current level of spending on nuclear weapons is unnecessary and unsustainable. We live in 2014, not 1980. The world is a very different place, and we need to plan accordingly."

This type of argument—advocating for a drastic reduction of nuclear weapons for moral and financial reasons—is being made not only in the United States. Retired Air Force general Bernard Norlain made this argument in 2011. (France is the fourth largest nuclear power after the United States, Russia,

250

and China.) General Norlain began by recalling the progress of the Reykjavík Summit. During the Cold War, "nearly 70,000 nuclear weapons of all types were produced. The number of such weapons has decreased to around 25,000, which is still enough to destroy the planet." And he wondered, "Is this devastating power still adapted to the world we know and does it follow the same strategic rules as those of the Cold War? . . . Faced with the threats of the 21st century, the strategic relevance of nuclear deterrence seems to be weakening." He continues his argument by referring to the dogma: of deterrence: "Not an official discourse that begins with a genuflection before the altar of deterrence, adding the inevitable mantra: 'We cannot uninvent nuclear.' But the altar is empty and we continue to spend billions while our armies have urgent needs. It is no longer strategy but theology."

General Norlain then listed the cost of nuclear weapons in the nine countries that have nuclear arsenals, who together "will spend $1 trillion in nuclear weapons over the next ten years. The United States spends $34 billion to $64 billion a year, with France paying between $4.7 billion and $6 billion depending on whether direct or indirect costs are considered. The official French figure is $3.5 billion a year."

The general had already led a forum on nuclear disarmament in 2009, along with two former French foreign ministers, Alain Juppé and Michel Rocard, and former defense minister Alain Richard. He went even further in his criticism that echoed the views of Senator Feinstein. "This weapon has become too dangerous for the planet. Dangerous, it has always been, but in a world divided into two blocs where the two players have clashed rather rationally. The effectiveness of this system was based on a small number of actors. But in an open world, where the emergence of new strategic actors makes the rules of the game more complex and fleeting, nuclear weapons, after playing a role of stability, become a source of destructive instability for the planet."

As to the risks of accidents, terrorist attacks, or proliferation, "though proliferation has been slow since we have gone from five to nine nuclear countries, if we do nothing the emergence of new actors, will lead to [an accelerating pace of] nuclear armament under the equalizing power of the atom."

There is therefore a profound danger that nuclear weapons will spread, and these weapons must absolutely not fall into the hands of irrational actors who obey nothing but their own irrationality. The danger is not only proliferation, but that routine deployment of nuclear weapons could also remove the sense of the ultimate lethality of these weapons, so that their use could become more of a simple extension of any unresolved conventional conflict. For the moment, fortunately, the doctrine of major power deterrence has been, and still remains, that of absolute nonuse of nuclear weapons. The fear of most nuclear experts, however, is that this doctrine has already begun to move from deterrence—passing upwards from the weak to the strong—to its reverse, with movement from the strong to the weak—or the mad. As the political scientist Pierre Hassner put it, "the notion of deterrence between the strong and the weak leads to a logic of use, even first use."

What measures must be taken, given the risks, to prevent the partial or total destruction of the planet?

"There is no alternative but to eliminate these weapons," says Hassner. "All negotiations on the reduction, deployment and alerting of these weapons are necessary, but they will be effective only if their goal is to achieve the objective of complete elimination. After all, this would only be the implementation of Article VI of the Treaty on the Non-Proliferation of Nuclear Weapons."

Though Barack Obama formulated this goal in Prague as early as 2009, since then, the US government has been taking precisely the opposite steps. France, the fourth-ranking nuclear power, is "opposed to this objective," according to Bernard Norlain. "It is therefore isolated in the international and European context," he concludes because, unlike France, all other European nations are anxious to end the existence of nuclear weapons on the planet. Apparently sheltered behind a new Maginot line, which provided little deterrent value to Nazi forces at the start of World War II, this French doctrine makes nuclear weapons the unbreachable core of its security. "Today the need is urgent to consider a new perspective on the security of every nuclear power, so it is time to open the debate by agreeing that the nuclear weapon is no longer the alpha and the omega of our security."

Bernard Norlain is a member of the "Stop the Bomb" association—a campaign to mobilize citizens willing to press for the elimination of nuclear weapons. Indeed, how will this goal ever be achieved if each individual does not take responsibility for its success? Another renowned French official, former minister of defense under François Mitterrand Paul Quilès, joined this Stop the Bomb movement. He explained his conversion to *La Revue Civique* in May 2013. "As regards nuclear weaponry, which is an integral part of the armaments wielded by the Minister of Defense, I've made several observations. In particular, I understood how speeches on this subject, by the President and his ministers, were prepared with the help of military experts and industrialists. I was also confronted by the famous military-industrial lobby, denounced by Eisenhower when he left the White House in 1961. I discovered all this, but at the same time I was the minister responsible for the application of a doctrine, at this time of the Cold War that was based on nuclear deterrence.

"And then, at the time of the fall of the Berlin Wall in 1989, I heard François Mitterrand wonder about the nature and role of a strategic weapon," Quilès recalls. "It must be said that his argument was lost in the different evolutionary concepts of the French doctrine: strategic, pre-strategic, tactical, weapon of non-employment. . . . I recall [Mitterrand's] outrageous reaction when a general explained to him that Germany could be a target from the East. I was a little surprised to find that the President of the Republic, the only individual with the power to launch a nuclear weapon since such a decree was issued in January 1964 by General de Gaulle, did not have all the elements essential to an understanding of this question. In any case, this was the origin of the decision to end deployment of the tactical Pluto missile. In 1995, Jacques Chirac decided to resume nuclear tests, just a few days before the fiftieth anniversary of the bombing of Hiroshima, though such tests had been halted since 1992. This created a very lively reaction in France and in the rest of the world. The Socialist Party called for a public debate, which took place in December 1995. It was the first (and only) debate on nuclear deterrence that had ever taken place on the floor of the National Assembly. That day, in my speech to the parliament and the gallery, after questioning the relevance of deterrence, I made a clear stand in favor of nuclear de-escalation."

At the international level, several organizations are leading the battle for nuclear denuclearization. The foremost of these organization is ICAN, the International Campaign Against Nuclear weapons. Founded in 2007 and based in Geneva, Switzerland, ICAN and its affiliates around the world won the Nobel Peace Prize of 2017 for their "work to draw attention to the catastrophic humanitarian consequences of any use of nuclear weapons and for its ground-breaking efforts to achieve a treaty-based prohibition of such weapons."

ICAN emphasizes that nuclear states should feel ashamed for possessing and manufacturing nuclear weapons. It works on the ground, with an army of volunteers, to rally the public opinion in the fight. After all, biological and chemical weapons have been banned. Why can't nuclear weapons be?

It's with that strong conviction that the organization launched an effort to have an international treaty to forever ban nuclear weapons, negotiated at the United Nations level. The treaty was finally settled and signed by the first countries in July 2017 at the UN headquarters in New York. As of January 2019, seventy countries have signed it and nineteen of them have ratified it. In total, according to ICAN, 120 governments support the nuclear ban—some of these are in the process of signing or ratifying. Unsurprisingly, the nine nuclear states—United States, Russia, China, France, United Kingdom, India, Pakistan, Israel, and North Korea—are opposed to the treaty.

"ICAN is an organization that has worked on nuclear summits for a long time, so the ideas behind the campaign were nothing new," explains Beatrice Fihn, executive director of ICAN, "But there was a recognition that civil society was quite spread out and people were focusing on very different things. And not so unified.

"Civil society has learned from campaigns to abolish land mines, for example. That working together in a coordinated way was much more effective. Based on that, and realizing there was no such coordination about nuclear weapons, ICAN was started. And there was always the idea about a treaty. But in the beginning, there was focus on the nuclear states. That the nuclear states would, one day, say yes to negotiating a treaty on nuclear disarmament.

"Gradually, the campaign moving along, the focus was put more on humanitarian consequences of nuclear weapons. And looking at these other treaties (the land mines treaty, the cluster munitions) as a normative issue (treaties on the prohibition of chemical and biological weapons) the campaign started coming around that we could prohibit nuclear weapons, without the nuclear states being on board. This lack of prohibition of nuclear weapons in the legal international framework, that's the problem. We banned all the other weapons which have indiscriminate inhumane impact on civilians, but we forgot to ban nuclear weapons. That's what we need to do as a first step, in order to have the nuclear states ultimately wanting to disarm.

"So that was the strategy of ICAN. To bring a change of perception. Because it is seen as a guarantee of security, as something powerful that the big powers have to have in order to feel safe. A prohibition can help change how we see nuclear weapons, from something seen as positive to something negative. When you can get people and government to think that nuclear weapons are inhumane, it's uncomfortable and it's not something you want to be associated with. Then disarmament is going to be easier.

"The deterrence issue, in many ways, reminds us of the gun debate in the United States. There are facts that say that if you have guns at home you are more likely to get shot. It makes all unsafe. It's the same with nuclear weapons, people feel they are safe. You're powerful with weapons. It's a very emotional argument. It doesn't always matter if you have logic. It's a feeling. And it's a feeling you can change by showing the reality of the weapons. The same way as the high school kids from Florida, when they were talking about the experience of being shot. That's how you change the perception of heavy guns. With nuclear weapons, we tell the stories of Hiroshima, Nagasaki, and all the nuclear test sites. And the impact. What happens to bodies, to your skin. The radiations. If you survive. Then it becomes very difficult to make these arguments about deterrence.

"The nuclear states are still reluctant to acknowledge the treaty. They put pressure on other countries who want to sign and ratify it. For us, it's evidence that it is working. Why pressuring African countries or Pacific Islands countries? They know that this is going to be the new norm that takes place. We also see people within the countries. In the public and the local level, people are supportive of this treaty. Like the state of California, which adopted a motion supporting the treaty. Some cities as well, like Baltimore and Los Angeles. We had some representatives at the House signing the ICAN pledge. A new reality is emerging as the people don't accept nuclear weapons anymore. We're hoping to make it difficult for these countries to continue to have and produce new nuclear weapons unchallenged.

"There are a lot of people making a lot of money on the modernization of these weapons. We had some great success around the world targeting private firms. One major Japanese bank decided to stop financing that. Companies should feel shame and not pride in financing that. We also know that these companies have difficulties recruiting new young scientists, in a similar way that tobacco companies now have difficulties in hiring. Because people don't want to be associated with it.

"With political, financial and cultural change, you can shift the entire way to talk about these weapons and the entire way to talk about what's acceptable and what's not. Of course, it's a long-term work. But if you think of how the smoking ban emerged, it's become the new normal. Today it looks so weird that someone would smoke a cigarette or start that. We can shift the culture."

That determination to shift the international conversation about nuclear weapons is not only meeting opposition in theory. It is also coming up against the reality of a world that has drastically changed since the Reykjavik Summit, and even more so in recent years. Vladimir Putin's foreign policy and the uncertainty of Donald Trump's diplomacy is making most international relations experts nervous. The nuclear risk seems higher today, in 2019, than it has in the last several decades.

One reason is Donald Trump's announcement of his wish to withdraw the United States from the INF Treaty, effectively abrogating the treaty unilaterally. The INF Treaty is that same treaty on intermediate nuclear missiles that was negotiated and agreed upon in Reykjavík by Ronald Reagan and Mikhail Gorbachev and signed in 1987. Announced by the president of the United States in October 2018, the decision to withdraw was explained by the fact that "Russia violates the treaty."

"It makes no sense for the United States to remain in a treaty that constrains our ability to respond to Russia's violations," said Secretary of State Mike Pompeo at a NATO meeting on December 4, 2018. "We hope that they'll change course, but there's been absolutely no indication that they'll do so." Moscow has denied violating the treaty and says it will continue to adhere to the treaty.[1] Moscow has denied violating the INF treaty, but as of February 2019, Russia decided to pull out in direct response to the American withdrawal.

Despite Trump's declaration, it is unclear whether the president alone can abrogate a treaty without Congress's approval—the Constitution says nothing about it, and the issue is much broader than just the US-Russia relationship right now. In a detailed *New York Times* article from December 9, 2018, David E. Sanger and William J. Broad explain that "the United States and Russia no longer have a monopoly on the missiles that Ronald Reagan and Mikhail Gorbachev agreed in 1987 to ban . . . Today, China relies on similar missiles for 95% of its ground-based fleet, and Iran, India, Saudi Arabia, North Korea and Taiwan are among the ten states with similar fast-growing arsenals." Admiral Harry B. Harris Jr., the US ambassador to South Korea and former commander of the American forces in the Pacific, said that "we are being taken to the cleaners by countries that are not signatories" of the INF Treaty. "The treaty," he said, "restricts the United States from building a new class of conventional and nuclear weapons to counter China's growing influence in the Pacific, while Beijing, the adversary it now worries about the most, faces no such limits."

George Shultz, the secretary of state in office in the Reagan administration, worries as well. He told the *New York Times*, "now is not the time to build larger arsenals of nuclear weapons. Now is the time to rid the world of this threat. Leaving the INF Treaty would be a huge step backward. We should fix it, not kill it."

The last word belongs to Beatrice Fihn of ICAN. This lawyer and executive director in her thirties joins the ninety-eight-year-old Shultz in a chorus of wisdom. "The risk of use, whether intentional or accidental, is higher today. Not just because of the current leaders. But also because we have more nuclear states and a very tense and unpredictable security situation in the world. And you have this kind of leaders walking back from these human rights, humanitarian law, international law, in general. Which is a dangerous trend that worries me," she says.

But there is more: "You have the combination of nuclear weapons and new technologies, such as artificial intelligence or cyberwarfare that is going to change the way the military operates in the future. And the impact of that on nuclear weapons can be very dangerous if we don't address these issues right now. Leaving this kind of 1945 technology, that are very clumsy and dangerous into a new military where things are preprogrammed, where the decision making is sped up, where we don't know where the information is coming from, or it can be hacked. . . . there is definitely a higher risk now," Fihn worries.

To end on a more positive note, the Nobel Peace Prize recipient underscores that "the fact that so many countries have signed on the nuclear ban treaty, is a huge step forward for the world. Each time a new country does, they sign on something that bans nuclear weapons forever and that's never been done before. And that's huge progress. Despite all the complications in the world right now, we have 120 governments that support this treaty (some of them are in the process to sign). It is a success that so many countries think that nuclear weapons are the wrong idea. We always focus on the nine countries who think they're a positive thing, but we forget that the rest of the world is getting momentum very strongly that nuclear weapons are simply unacceptable."[2]

# *Epilogue*

◆

An awesome silence, broken only by the distant purr of a helicopter descending from a high altitude. We raise our heads. We look at the sky—blue and clear. Then we close our eyes to imagine what it must have been like on August 6, 1945, at 8:15 A.M., when the first atomic bomb fell here. The Memorial Park of Peace is located in the heart of Hiroshima. At its northern end, the ruins of the Dome building recall what happened that day.

The park is closed to the public on May 27, 2016. The flame burns in silence. It will not be extinguished until there are no nuclear bombs left on Earth. The Ark of Peace, a large white sculpture, is placed in line with the flame and the dome, behind a long basin. Opposite, a reviewing stand with some fifty guests has been installed. On the left side, in three well-defined areas, some 300 Japanese and international journalists. Everyone is waiting. Not a sound disrupts what resembles a meditation session.

Five fifteen in the evening. Light is beginning to fade, but the temperature remains warm, comforting. The presidential convoy has just arrived at the other end of the park. A few minutes pass, still with this same impressive calm. Finally, Barack Obama and Shinzo Abe walk together, side by side, up the central aisle. The president of the United States and the prime minister of Japan climb the seven steps. They move slowly towards the central arch. Obama looks discreetly at a mark on the ground, which tells him where to stand. Two Japanese children, a girl and a boy, approach carrying a wreath of white flowers. The American takes it and turns, walking a few steps to lay the wreath in front of the monument. He retreats, then with his hands folded in front of him, reflects briefly, silently. His face shows no emotion, yet is marked by a certain gravity. Then Obama returns to his place. It is now Shinzo Abe's turn to perform the same ritual. The cameras crackle. NHK, Japanese public television, is broadcasting live and does not miss a single gesture of the two men.

Barack Obama and Shinzo Abe shake hands. No effusive words. Just a handshake, a look straight in the eyes. A striking image of American-Japanese reconciliation. Especially in this symbolic setting. This is a historic moment. Barack Obama is the first sitting president of the United States to visit the martyr city of Hiroshima. Seventy-one years have passed since the B-29 Enola Gay dropped "Little Boy" on the Japanese city: thirty-three tons of TNT as a trigger and 141 pounds of uranium 235 that killed some 140,000 people.

"We have known the horrors and agony of war. May we find the courage, together, to spread peace and build a world without nuclear weapons," the American president writes in the reception book of the memorial. Obama, taking advantage of a trip to Japan for a G7 summit, has traveled to Hiroshima with the goal of reaffirming his message from Prague. His speech at the Memorial Park does not apologize to the Japanese people. But he insists on the horror of war, the necessary reconciliation, and the moral responsibility of the nuclear powers to face up to technical progress. And thus to eliminate nuclear weapons.

A man and a woman listen to the President's speech with the utmost attention. Placed in the third row, just in front of Obama, Toshiharu and Yorie Kano are among the dozen of Hiroshima survivors invited by the White House to attend the ceremony. Brother and sister, they say they are "moved to be here."

"It was not necessary to apologize. Merely his presence here, his recognition of the victims, is already highly powerful in itself and has exceptional value. It was time. And now it's time to move forward," says Yorie Kano.

Toshiharu and Yorie have a singular history. They are the two survivors of Hiroshima who were closest to the epicenter—the very place where the bomb exploded—just 800 yards north of the dome, in the city center. Yorie was three years old when the bomb destroyed the city. Her father, Toshiyuki Kano, was a colonel in the Japanese army. The barracks of the troops he led were not far away. His wife, Shinzue, cared for the house and her two children: Yorie and her little brother, who was one year old. Shinzue was also three months pregnant with a third child on that August day.

Shortly after eight in the morning, on August 6, when Japanese children went off to school and adults went to work, Toshiyuki looked up at the sky. He heard the sound of the engine of a B-29, the American flying fortresses that had been pounding Japan since November 1944. Tokyo had been on fire after repeated bombings since April. However, Toshiyuki saw nothing that morning. But a presentiment made him uncomfortable. "Stay at home!" he ordered his wife and children. He decided to go on foot to his barracks.

In the sky over Hiroshima, the Enola Gay appeared. The American aircraft was accompanied by two escorts, which would depart and then return to take pictures and measurements from the air. For what was about to take place was hardly a classic bombing run.

At 8:09 A.M., Captain Paul Tibbetts wheeled his B-52 into his bombing run and turned control over to his bombardier, Major Thomas Ferebee who released "Little Boy" at 8:15. The forty-four second fall of the first atomic bomb was slowed by a parachute, to allow time for the Enola Gay to move rapidly away.

Little Boy exploded, as planned, at 1900 feet, before reaching the surface—an air burst above the city center of Hiroshima, designed to do as much damage over as wide a field as possible.

The flash was instantaneous. The blast of the explosion threw Toshiyuki Kano flat on the street. Little Yorie, in the drawing room, was buried under the floor of the house, which was at first lifted, then collapsed onto itself. Nobody understood what was going on. It took many minutes to realize that this was not a usual bomb. There was the extent of destruction. There was the smell. And there were bodies in flames, burned alive by the intense heat. Absolute horror.

"It's a miracle we survived," Yorie says today. She cannot really explain it. Her little brother died at the age of one-and-a-half. But her second brother, Toshiharu, would be born six months later, in an environment of total desolation. Today he is a man of seventy-one, proud of his samurai grandfather, Toshiharu.

The family moved to Tokyo a few years later, then immigrated to the United States and settled in Utah. Toshiharu, or Tosh, still lives there. Yorie, meanwhile, settled in California. "I chose not to have a child," she says. "All my life as a young woman, I heard that I was in danger of giving birth to a malformed child." As for Tosh, he had a son. "I can tell you that when he was born, it was a huge relief to see that he was well constituted. It is a psychological trauma to live with this pressure."

Their mother, Shinzue, lived until the age of ninety-three. But their father died at the age of sixty-two, of pancreatic cancer—a classic illness among those who had been irradiated. "I've had health troubles all my life, including tuberculosis," says Toshiharu. Thinking back to his childhood, passed mainly in Tokyo after the family left Hiroshima, Tosh cannot hold back his tears. "I missed school so often, because I was regularly sick. I was very late. It was hard to keep up with the pace," he explains, stressing the harshness of the Japanese school system. "I felt pressured all the time."

Tosh and Yorie's grandfather was a samurai. The code of honor, value, work were an integral part of the daily lives of the children. "I tried to commit suicide several times," confesses Toshiharu, still in tears. My father said, "You're weak, you cannot even kill yourself." He ended up as a civil engineer in Salt Lake City.

Surprisingly, he managed to escape death twice, once saved from drowning and another time failing to catch a plane that later crashed. "I feel invested with a mission," he admits. "I am living in spite of all this, and I carry a message of peace." It was very important for him to convey the family's history in a book he cowrote with his wife.

When the White House announced at the end of April 2016 that Barack Obama would go to Hiroshima, Yorie and Tosh were seized with emotion. "It was high time," said Yorie. "This is not most important, that he apologizes," says Toshiharu. "The most important thing is this gesture he shared with the Japanese Prime Minister. And that we fight for a world without nuclear weapons." He promised, it is his mission: to hammer this message of peace.

May 27, 2016, was the first time Tosh had returned to Hiroshima since the age of two. Yorie, for her part, had not been back there for forty-five years. It was a historical and personally moving moment for these two survivors, who bear dual nationality and pledge that their experience must be not be repeated. Never again.

# Yesterday, Today, and Tomorrow

## by David A. Andelman

The roots of the fall of Communism, the end of a monolithic Soviet empire, and the rise of an American supremacy that lasted until the debut of the Trump years were laid during those days Reagan and Gorbachev spent together in Reykjavik. Much of this did not truly come together for me until years later, however, until I looked back, long before Reykjavik, to Reagan's first inauguration.

I'd joined CBS News from *The New York Times* shortly after the election of 1980 and was spending a few months in New

York learning network television before heading abroad to my post in Paris. On January 19, 1981, as the greenest of CBS correspondents, I was shipped down to Washington and assigned as the network pool correspondent for the Reagan inaugural. CBS had drawn the short straw and was the pool network for the entire inaugural day, which meant assigning a correspondent and crew to follow the new President from the moment he left Blair House in the morning until we tucked him back into the White House following the last of twelve inaugural balls that evening. The pool correspondent, however would never get on the air unless the President got shot.

So, the evening before, having no assigned task, I invited my old Harvard professor, Richard Pipes, to dinner at a K Street restaurant. Pipes, who'd been designated as chief Soviet advisor on Reagan's National Security Council, spent much of the dinner berating the Soviets for treating him most shabbily when he went over to do research, especially in the Lenin Library. There, each researcher was given a cubicle and waited for the material he'd requested to show up from the stacks. Invariably, Pipes fumed, "they'd wheel by a cart groaning under a load of documents, books for [Columbia Professor Marshal] Shulman. For me, there was one thin folder, if that." Pipes never got past those slights.

At the end of our dinner, over coffee, Pipes finally leaned over and whispered, "Let me tell you something else." He paused for dramatic effect. "Sometime in the next eight years. . . ." I shot back, "My, you are optimistic. Tomorrow is just the start of Reagan's first four-year term." Without even acknowledging my caveat, he pressed on. "Sometime in the next eight years, we will be bringing an end to Communism in the Soviet Union." I was aghast at his audacity. And how would he do that exactly? At the time, Communism and the Soviet Union looked like the thousand-year Reich—all but invincible. But Pipes thought he knew differently. He smiled at me. "We are going to spend them to death." Basically, Pipes had figured out this was the only way to beat the Soviets and end Communism. It was not until the Communist system finally began to unravel barely three years after that fateful summit in Reykjavik that I reflected back on those words of Richard Pipes.

I became persuaded that at least in some quarters this could have been an underlying reason for pursuing Reagan's Star Wars program that turned out to be quite quixotic. Reagan, persuaded of its viability, could never give it up in Reykjavik, and there were many, like Pipes, who were quite favorably disposed toward its pursuit. Pipes, in his view, saw it as an integral part of a much larger, grander, certainly more ambitious plan. Gorbachev and the Soviets knew they could never hope to match Star Wars, with its vast scientific and industrial scope and especially its expense. Many around Reagan knew secretly that it would never work. And indeed to this day such a concept never really has. But at least some of the Reagan inner circle really did not care. Star Wars, as they saw it, would eventually accomplish its most fundamental and awesome purpose—bringing an end to the

Communist experiment, leaving America as the only surviving superpower.

Still, while Reykjavik failed to produce the agreement on, or chart a path toward, the zero-nuclear world that Gorbachev sought, it did lead to other, more modest but no-less-enduring nuclear pacts, along two tracks that have stood the test of time. Intermediate range nuclear (INF) missiles were originally based in Europe but, with the proliferation of nuclear forces in Asia and South Asia, now pose a series of global and regional challenges. Intercontinental ballistic missiles (ICBMs) are largely the domain of the United States and Russia. These were at the heart of the Cold War standoff and the often tense peace guaranteed by the doctrine of Mutually Assured Destruction (MAD)—if you launch your weapons at us, you may be guaranteed that we will have the second-strike capacity to launch ours, with equal devastation, at you.

These were the kinds of threats that a succession of East-West negotiations from the early 1970s to the early 2000s were designed to diminish and, ultimately, prevent. The most immediate result of Reykjavik was the Intermediate Range Nuclear Forces (INF) treaty, signed December 8, 1987, whose provisions eliminated all ground-launched ballistic and cruise missiles with ranges from 500 to 5,500 kilometers. But its principal, really precedent-shattering provision was an intrusive system of on-site inspections, which laid the groundwork for the verification of the START I treaty that arrived six years later, cutting ICBM weapons, and eventually New Start, which is still in force. These successive treaties have slashed the number of deployed warheads from 6,000 under START I to 1,550 today—more than enough, in either case, to do away with all life on earth. Still, each narrower number reduced the prospects of a horrific accident.

All these treaties did fail in one critical respect—halting the spread of nuclear weapons to new, less rational powers in less stable regions. India and Pakistan provide their own meta-stability under the MAD doctrine, though Pakistan's close ties to terrorist organizations such as the Taliban raise ever more dangerous questions as to unchecked proliferation challenges. China has joined Russia and the United States, becoming effectively a member of what is now a nuclear triad of MAD. Add, as well, France and the United Kingdom, each with its own nuclear arsenal, and NATO members Belgium, Germany, Italy, the Netherlands, and Turkey, where nuclear arms are based or stored. But teetering in the wings are North Korea and Iran, and, should either of them become a full-fledged nuclear power, Saudi Arabia or any other nearby nation with the resources or the will to field their own deliverable nuclear arms. Imagine a nuclear-armed Nigeria (Africa's most populous nation) or Persian Gulf sheikdoms facing down not only Iran but Israel, whose nuclear arsenal has never been either acknowledged nor, for that matter, doubted. Japan and South Korea could certainly aspire to field a nuclear arsenal in the face of a nuclear-armed North Korea.

So where we stand today is a far more complex world than the one Reagan and Gorbachev sought to pick their way through more than three decades ago. It takes wise leaders on every side to master what is rapidly becoming a three-dimensional chess game of existential consequences. Sadly, this does not appear to be the case.

Donald Trump, who arrived with his tortured sense of East-West rivalry and American supremacy, has suddenly and arbitrarily announced his intention to pull out of the centerpiece of the process launched in Reykjavik and that has stood the test of time so admirably. When Trump announced his decision to withdraw from the INF treaty after the six-month window provided, Vladimir Putin took the opportunity to bolt from the treaty himself. Each side charged the other with blatant violations, and with some justification. Still, the scrapping of the entire, carefully-constructed framework is hardly a path toward the nuclear-free future that Gorbachev and Reagan had discussed three decades ago. Instead, it seems likely that a new arms race has been ignited, based on new and potentially more lethal weaponry than either Reagan or Gorbachev could have imagined.

Now, however, for perhaps the first time in its history, Russia actually has the capacity to match or even surpass American missile technology and deployments. Which is why the withdrawal of the United States from the INF treaty is so deeply troubling and hardly likely to accomplish what Gorbachev had set out to accomplish in Reykjavik—containing the American ability to dominate the Soviet Union. Instead, Vladimir Putin really does believe, and perhaps with some justification, that today's Russia has the capacity to match or even surpass America's military-industrial complex.

All these titanic shifts make the existing arms limitation agreements all the more essential—far more so than in the long-ago era when they were negotiated. But withdrawing from any such treaty also requires a deep understanding of the consequences of these negotiations and particularly the potential inherent in their undoing.

The arms limitation agreements that were negotiated in the pre-Trump era were based on several critical elements. First was the apparently equal ability and will of each side to contain a race toward strategic superiority that each recognized could be won by neither. Then there was the acceptance that none of these agreements was being negotiated or maintained in a vacuum. The United States had nuclear-armed allies across Europe that were equally committed both to enforcing a nuclear reduction regime and preventing the spread of nuclear weapons to nations like Iran. While all of these tenets are still held by America's allies, none of these concepts are apparently recognized or accepted by Donald Trump.

How can we possibly expect Europe to respect us if we do not respect anything that Europe stands for—especially the great pillars of the East-West relationship of which these nuclear pacts are a deeply held foundation? Yet Donald Trump has no interest in being respected or dependent on any traditional ally. He is persuaded that the American military-industrial complex can out-spend, out-innovate, out-produce, and out-deploy any enemy or any ally for that matter. And, by the way, in the Trump geopolitical lexicon, Russia is also no longer America's enemy.

Sadly, the fallout might long outlast the Trump era. With Russia withdrawn from the INF treaty, scrapping New Start could be not far behind. The consequences of such actions by both parties today are even more horrific than any that might have been imagined when Reagan and Gorbachev were discussing the prospects of a world without nukes. It is also eminently worth examining this new world that today is so different from the one envisioned by both the United States and the Soviet Union back then.

In February 2019, Vladimir Putin, speaking in the shadow of the Kremlin, outlined the shape of such a new world in his annual state-of-the-nation address. His threat was direct and accompanied by a vast and deep command of the history of East-West arms control. In 2001, he recalled, President George W. Bush pulled out of the Anti-Ballistic Missile Treaty signed by Richard Nixon and Leonid Brezhnev in 1972. At the time, in a Rose Garden statement, Bush declared, "I have concluded the ABM treaty hinders our government's ability to develop ways to protect our people from future terrorist or rogue state missile attack. Defending the American people is my highest priority and I cannot and will not allow the United States to remain in a treaty that prevents us from developing effective defenses." Eighteen years later, Donald Trump used nearly identical language in pulling out of the INF treaty.

"You didn't listen to our country then," Putin said in 2019. "Listen to us now." Behind him flashed video and animations of next-generation ICBMs, nuclear-powered hypersonic cruise missiles, underwater drones, and other devices Russia had developed in the wake of the end of the ABM treaty and that it now felt free to deploy. Then Putin elaborated: "Russia will be forced to create and deploy new types of weapons that could be used not only against the territories where a direct threat to us comes from, but also against the territories where decision-making centers directing the use of missile systems threatening us are located. The capability of such weapons, including the time to reach those centers, will be equivalent to the threats against Russia."

Indeed, with Communism dead, the new pseudo-capitalist Russia is a more formidable enemy by far and, as Putin suggested, in a position to make good on threats once viewed as largely empty bluster from his Kremlin predecessors. The United States has similar weapons under development, including hypersonic weapons able to travel nine times the speed of sound and largely impervious to any existing missile defense systems. American officials have conceded, however, that, while working diligently on such advances, the United States is years away from testing and deployment.

Despite all of Trump's braggadocio of undertaking "the greatest military buildup ever," the United States seems suddenly to find itself in the deeply uncomfortable and utterly unprecedented position of playing catch-up in an arms race where Russia is calling the shots. At the same time, it leaves America's longtime closest allies questioning the value of counting on a nuclear umbrella controlled by an utterly unpredictable and irrational partner, whose military-industrial leadership has been usurped by their most pernicious enemy. It is little wonder that European leaders are moving toward creation of a European defense force. Once lost, the lead in any arms contest is only regained with enormous difficulty and colossal cost.

Moreover, by withdrawing from the INF treaty and threatening to pull out of New Start, Trump has removed twin, parallel umbrellas of security that have stood the test of time over decades. And at the same time he has raised fears in Europe, which has seen itself protected for decades by the INF treaty and in the United States, shielded from unchecked ICBM deployment under New Start. Indeed Putin, in his 2019 remarks, seemed to be making a major effort to reassure Western Europe, which he is anxious to split from NATO, that he is retargeting the new generation of missiles on the United States.

Abrogating one treaty or set of treaties raises the necessity of either beginning again from scratch on new arms control talks or bolting headlong into an utterly enervating, prospectively deadly, new arms race than can serve no purpose and protect no nation. I can still recall camping with my television crew for endless weeks next to the estate on the outskirts of Geneva where negotiators argued interminably over how many nuclear warheads or what "throw weight" could dance on the head of a missle. Such debates stretched on year after fruitless year. Major arms control agreements are never lightly arrived at nor, if casually dismissed, easily revisited.

*An Impossible Dream* outlines some of the pitfalls of failing to look multiple moves ahead. Our only hope is that today's leaders will be wise enough to understand the value of what has come before and not rush precipitously over the brink into an unknown and likely quite perilous future without a single safety net of international accords.

# Acknowledgments

More than two years of work were necessary to carry this project from the beginning to its release in France, in October 2016. I want to thank my publisher and everyone at L'Archipel, in Paris, who believed in the topic and made it possible. The American part of the adventure started with David A. Andelman, whom I met in New York and who agreed to translate the French manuscript into English. David also put me in touch with Alexis Hurley, at InkWell Management, who became my agent. Many, many thanks to both of them. Of course, I can't thank Jessica Case and Claiborne Hancock at Pegasus enough. They picked up the book to make it a reality in the United States and the English-speaking market.

I want to particularly thank Mikhail Gorbachev, who met with me at his foundation in Moscow, for supporting the project and accepting to write an introduction for the English edition. This meeting was made possible by Pavel Palazchenko, who gave me access to important sources as well.

In the United States, I thank everyone at the Ronald Reagan Presidential Library in Simi Valley, California, and in particular national archivist Ray Wilson, who was a precious help during my months of research.

Thank you to Svetlana Savranskaya at George Washington University, who granted me access to important Soviet sources.

Also, this book wouldn't have been possible without the people who agreed to be interviewed, giving life to the tale: John Poindexter, George Shultz, Patrick Buchanan, Josef Schwartz, Pavel Palazchenko, Roald Sagdeev, Bernard Norlain, and Paul Quiles.

Thank you to my family and my friends, with a special mention to Julia Gallucci for her particular input and support.

I have a specific thought for Andre Kaspi, my US history teacher at the Sorbonne University in Paris; for Francoise Thom, an expert on the Soviet Union at the same university; and for Jean-Marie Cavada, my first "boss" as a journalist: working with him in my early years was the best training for a passionate and rigorous journalistic life.

I want to also acknowledge Tosh and Yorie Kamo, who had the grace and the courage to come back to Hiroshima with me, and Major Myles Caggins, of the National Security Council under President Obama, who made possible that rendezvous with history in Japan.

Last, but not least, thank you to the following people who financially supported the English translation process through an online fundraising campaign in 2017: Iris and David Strauss, Michel and Barbara Karsky, Marie-Nadia Karsky, Fabienne Serina-Karsky, Carri Levinson-Daly, Jean-Christophe Bornaghi, Cecile Balavoine, Paul Marchand, Florence Boulin, Horst Kramer, Truls Bjorvik, Corinne Valette, Dominique and Nicole Serina, Delphine Serina, Elisabeth Nataf, Olivier Buisson, Nicolas Gotchac, David and Armelle Opoczynski, Veronique Dupont, Arielle Abbou, and Cecile Le Roy.

# Sources

**Interviews with the author:**

John Poindexter, December 17, 2013.
Roald Sagdeev, January 22, 2014.
Patrick Buchanan, December 27, 2013.
George Shultz, letter to the author, December 6, 2013.
Pavel Palazchenko, April 9, 2015
Jimmy Carter, letter to the author, September 2015.
Josef Schwartz, October 31, 2014.
Yorie Kano, May 27, 2016.

**Prologue**

*The Missileers*, Unfictional, produced by Eric Molinksy and Bob Carlson. KCRW. Aired on September 3rd 2013.

**Chapter 1: In the Reagan White House**

Kathryn Moore, *The American President, a Complete History*. Fall River 2007. www.foodtimeline.org/presidents.htm#reagan.
*Daily Operations meeting, Tuesday October 7, 1986 and Monday September 29, 1986*. Ronald Reagan Presidential Library.
Donald Regan Obituary. The Economist, June 19, 2003.
*White House confirms Reagans follow Astrology up to a point*. The New York Times, May 4, 1988.
Official biographic elements. Ronald Reagan Presidential Library. www .reaganfoundation.org

*Ronald Reagan played Informant role for FBI in 40s.* Chicago Tribune, August 26, 1985.

Documentary *Reagan*, "American Experience" series produced by WGBH Boston. Aired on PBS in 2008.

Jack Matlock, *Reagan and Gorbachev, How the Cold War ended*, Random House, 2004. p. 6.

Sarah McClendon, *Mr President, Mr President!*, General Publishing Group, 1996. p. 190.

## Chapter 2: Gorba . . . Who?

Patrice Gelard, *De Brejnev a Tchernenko et les dix-huit mois de Iouri Andropov*, Pouvoirs 33, 1985, p. 149 (in French).

Nicolas Werth, *Histoire de l'Union sovietique de Lenine a Staline (1917–1953)*, PUF Que Sais-je? 2013 pp.66–67; pp. 116-117 (in French).

Hubert Vedrine, *Les Mondes de Francois Mitterrand*, Fayard 1996. p. 371 (in French).

George Shultz, *Turmoil and Triumph, My years as Secretary of State*, Charles Scribner, 1989. pp. 526–527.

*Memorandum for the President, November 12, 1985.* Donald Regan Files, Box 5-7. Ronald Reagan Presidential Library. www.nobelprize .org and www.gorby.ru

Mikhail Gorbachev, *Mémoires*, Le Rocher, 1995. pp. 82–83; 183; 225; 363–364 (in French).

Pavel Palazchenko, *My years with Gorbachev and Shevardnadze, the Memoir of a Soviet Interpreter*, Penn State Press, 1997. p. 23.

## Chapter 3: First Meeting in Geneva

*Memorandum of conversation. Reagan–Gorbachev meetings in Geneva. First private meeting.* Jack Matlock Files, Box 57. Ronald Reagan Presidential Library.

*Memorandum of conversation. Reagan–Gorbachev meetings in Geneva. Second plenary meeting.* Jack Matlock Files, Box 57. Ronald Reagan Presidential Library.

Paul Lettow, *Ronald Reagan and His Quest to Abolish Nuclear Weapons*, Random House, 2005. p. 186.

Mikhail Gorbachev, *Mémoires*, p. 508 (in French).

## Chapter 4: The Nuclear Question

Robert Norris and Hans Kristensen, *Global Nuclear Weapons Inventories 1945–2010*, Bulletin of the Atomic Scientists, July-August 2010.

*President Reagan's trip to Reykjavik. Background book.* Jack Matlock notes. Ronald Reagan Presidential Library.

*Comparison of US and Soviet Nuclear and Space Talks positions, President Reagan's trip to Reykjavik. Background book.* Jack Matlock notes. Ronald Reagan Presidential Library.

NSC Executive Secretariat. Jack Matlock Files. Box 56. Ronald Reagan Presidential Library.

Bob Linhard, *Memorandum for Robert McFarlane, Draft NSDD on presenting the SDI Program*, April 15, 1985. Sven Kraemer Files. Ronald Reagan Presidential Library.

*French Position on military use of space, June 11, 1984.* Jack Matlock Files. Box 57. Ronald Reagan Presidential Library.

## Chapter 5: Reykjavík: The Preparations

Anatoly Chernaev, *My Six Years with Gorbachev*, Penn State Press, 2000. pp. 75; 77–78.

Mikhail Gorbachev, *Mémoires*, op.cit. p. 248 (in French).

*Excerpts from Gorbachev's Speech on Chernobyl Accident*, The New York Times, May 15 1986.

Jack Matlock, *Reagan and Gorbachev, How the Cold War Ended*, Random House 2004. pp. 188–189.

*Yuri Orlov, The End of an Ordeal*, Newsweek October 13, 1986.

*John Poindexter, Memorandum for the president. Lessons from the Daniloff case.* Jack Matlock Files. Box 57. Ronald Reagan Presidential Library.

*The Daniloff Scorecard.* Newsweek, October 13, 1986.

Gallup poll, 847 adults. October 1 and 2, 1986 published in Newsweek, October 13, 1986.

*Memorandum for the President through Donald T. Regan from William Henkel.* Jack Matlock Files. Box 56. Ronald Reagan Presidential Library.

*William Henkel to Donald T. Regan. "Summit II planning meeting," July 14, 1986.* Jack Matlock Files. Box 56. Ronald Reagan Presidential Library.

*Daily Operations meeting. Tuesday September 30, 1986.* Ronald Reagan Presidential Library.

U.S. Department of State, Bureau of Public Affairs. *Soviet noncompliance with arms control agreements, February 1, 1985.* Ronald Reagan Presidential Library.

*Confidential Fax Reykjavik: presidential visit: special mission team.* Jack Matlock Files, Box 57. Ronald Reagan Presidential Library.

*NSC, Directive number 244. October 3, 1986.* NSC Files. Ronald Reagan Presidential Library.

*Memorandum for the NSC staff, from Robert Pearson. Subject: presidential remarks, executive exchange commission.* NSC Files. Ronald Reagan Presidential Library.

*NSC Directive number 245. Goals and objectives of President's meeting with Gorbachev in Iceland.* NSC Files. Ronald Reagan Presidential Library.

*How to maximize your leverage. October 2, 1986.* NSC Files. Declassified in 2006. Ronald Reagan Presidential Library.

*Gorbachev's position on the eve of the summit, October 2, 1986.* Top Secret. Ronald Reagan Presidential Library.

Series of documents *The Soviet Preparation for Reykjavik: Four Documents.* Commented by historian David Holloway. Hoover Institution, Stanford University.

*V. Politburo TsK KPSS (1985-1991), Politburo minutes in Al'pina, Moscow 2006.* In The Reykjavik Files, National Security Archives, George Washington University.

*Series of Documents Kataev,* Box 1. Hoover Institution, Stanford University.

*Material on Nuclear-Space arms in preparation for the meeting with R. Reagan. Series of Documents Kataev,* Box 1. Hoover Institution, Stanford University.

*Notes from Bill Henkel, NSC Files.* Ronald Reagan Presidential Library.

## Chapter 6: Reykjavík, Day 1

All the quotes in this chapter and chapter 7 are extracted from two sources: one American source and one Soviet source. The content are almost fully identical:

*Memorandum of conversation. Reagan–Gorbachev meetings in Reykjavik.* Jack Matlock Files. Ronald Reagan Library.

*Conversations of M.S. Gorbachev with R. Reagan in Reykjavik on 11-12 October 1986.* Archives from the Gorbachev Foundation in

Moscow, translated in English by Svetlana Savranskaya and Thomas Blanton. National Security Archives. George Washington University.

George Shultz, *Turmoil and Triumph*, op. cit. p. 753.

Mikhail Gorbachev, *Mémoires*, op.cit., p. 523 (in French).

*Memorendum for Donald Regan from John Poindexter, Reykjavik Chronology*, October 18, 1986. Ronald Reagan Presidential Library.

George Shultz, *Turmoil and Triumph*, op.cit p. 762.

Anatoly Chernyaev, *My Six years with Gorbachev*, op. cit. p .86.

## Chapter 7: Reykjavík, Day 2

All the quotes in this chapter and in chapter 6 are taken from two sources, one American and one Soviet. The identical contents match perfectly. American source:

*Memorandum of conversation. Reagan-Gorbachev meetings in Reykjavik*. Jack Matlock Files. Ronald Reagan Library.

*Conversations of M.S. Gorbachev with R. Reagan in Reykjavik on 11-12 October 1986*. Archives from the Gorbachev Foundation in Moscow, translated in English by Svetlana Savranskaya and Thomas Blanton. National Security Archives. George Washington University.

Jack Matlock, *Reagan and Gorbachev*, op.cit. p. 232.

Mikhail Gorbachev, *Mémoires*, op.cit. p. 526 (in French).

Pavel Palazchenko, *My years with Gorbachev and Shevardnadze*, op.cit., p. 55.

Jack Matlock, *Reagan and Gorbachev*, op. cit. p. 236.

## Chapter 8: From Hangover to START

*Live from Reykjavik*, NBC News with Tom Brokaw, October 12, 1986. Ronald Reagan Presidential Library.

Mikhail Gorbachev, *Mémoires*, op. cit. p. 527 (in French).

*Reykjavik: Documents and Materials*. Novosti Press Agency Publishing House (in English). Moscow 1987.

*Interview of Admiral Poindexter on return from Iceland, Air Force One, Internal Transcript. October 12, 1986*. Ronald Reagan Files/ Iceland Summit, Box 5. Ronald Reagan Presidential Library.

*Pool Report: Air Force One—Keflavik Naval Air Force Base to Andrews Air Force Base. Sunday October 12, 1986, 7 p.m. EDT.* Ronald Regan Files/Iceland Summit, Box 5. Ronald Reagan Presidential Library.

Jack Matlock Files, Box 57. Ronald Reagan Presidential Library.

*Remarks by Chief of Staff Donald T. Regan, October 14, 1986*, Office of the Press secretary, Don Regan Files. Ronald Reagan Presidential Library.

*The Reagan-Gorbachev meeting in Reykjavik*, US Information agency, Foreign press center. Guest: Jack Matlock. Box 57. Ronald Reagan Presidential Library.

*Remarks by the President during briefing with network anchors and columnists, October 14, 1986.* Ronald Reagan Presidential Library.

*Memorandum for Ronald Reagan from Peter Roussel. October 15, 1986.* Ronald Reagan Presidential Library.

*Post-Summit tracking.* Ronald Reagan Presidential Library.

*Carter: Reagan Made Big Mistake in Arms Talks.* UPI, October 18, 1986.

United States Information Agency, Special Report. Foreign Media Reaction. *Conclusion of Pre-Summit Conference*, October 13, 1986.

The Gorbachev Foundation Archives: *Anatoly Chernaev's notes: Gorbachev's thoughts on Reykjavik, October 12, 1986.* Translated in English by Svetlana Savranskaya and Thomas Blanton. National Security Archives. George Washington University.

Anatoly Chernaev, *My Six Years with Gorbachev*, op. cit. pp.89–90.

Mikhail Gorbachev, *Mémoires*, op.cit. p. 529 (in French).

*Soviet and other foreign reactions in a zero-ballistic missile world*, National Intelligence Council, January 1987. Ronald Reagan Presidential Library.

*National Security Council. Memorandum for Franck C. Carlucci, from William Cockell. JCS Meeting with the president. January 5, 1987.* Ronald Reagan Presidential Library.

*Memorandum for the President, from Alton Keel. Top Secret until 2012. Initial JCS Report on eliminating ballistic missiles. December 18, 1986.* Ronald Reagan Presidential Library.

*Memorandum for the President, from John Poindexter, US-Soviet Relations: where do we go from here?* Ronald Reagan Presidential Library.

*Shultz recommended next steps post-Reykjavik. October 13, 1986.* Ronald Reagan Presidential Library.

*Memorandum for the President, Post–Reykjavik instructions for the Geneva negociators. October 19, 1986.* Ronald Reagan Presidential Library.

*Memorandum for the President, from John Poindexter, Why we can't commit to eliminating all nuclear weapons within 10 years. October 16, 1986.* Ronald Reagan Presidential Library.

Charles E. Bennett, *The Rush to Deploy SDI*. The Atlantic Monthly. April 1988.

## Chapter 9: A World Without Nuclear Bombs

New Start Treaty: www.state.gov/t/avc/newstart/index.htm.

*Obama, in Prague, Calls for Elimination of Nuclear Weapons.* Radio Free Europe/Radio Liberty. April 5, 2009.

Graham Allison, *Nuclear Terrorism, the Ultimate Preventable Catastrophe*, Times Books 2005.

*Alerte au terrorisme nucleaire*, Le Monde 2, March 19, 2005 (in French).

Eric Schlosser, *Command and Control, Nuclear Weapons, the Damascus Incident and the Illusion of Safety*. Penguin Books. 2013.

Conference by Eric Schlosser at KPCC Radio, Pasadena, October 7, 2013.

60 Minutes, CBS News. *Inside America's Missile Field*. April 25, 2014.

*New Nuclear Weapons Needed, Many Experts Say, Pointing to Aged Arsenal. Los Angeles Times*, November 29, 2014.

*Obama Inscreases Nuclear Weapons Production and Research*. Allgov. com. October 27, 2014.

*Senator Dianne Feinstein: America's Nuclear Arsenal is Unnecessary and Unsustainably Large*. Washington Post, December 3, 2014.

Bernard Norlain, *L'arme nucleaire est inutile et couteuse*, Le Monde, October 28, 2011 (in French).

Paul Quiles, *Nucleaire, un mensonge francais. Reflexions sur le desarmement nucleaire*. Editions Charles Leopold Mayer, 2012 (in French).

Toshiharu and Rita Kano, *Passport to Hiroshima*, Create Space, 2015.

1. Source: *Washington Post* "Trump administration gives Russia an ultimatum on Cold-War era arms treaty", December 4th 2018.
2. Interview with Beatrice Fihn, ICAN Executive Director. January 11th 2019

# Index

## P

package agreement, 158
Pakistan, 7, 243, 275
Palazchenko, Pavel, 53, 119–120, 143–145, 173–176, 226–228
Palmer, Mark, 58
parallel diplomacy, 79
Pearson, Robert, 95
*perestroika*, 52
Perle, Richard, 122, 140, 142, 202, 221
Permanent Consultative Commission, 69–70
Pershing II missiles, 20, 44, 72, 137
Pipes, Richard, 272–273
plutonium, 237, 249
Poindexter, John
  on Daniloff case, 90
  on outside influences, 104
  post-summit press conference by, 191–195
  on Reagan, 37–38, 181
  at Reykjavik Summit, 122–125, 139
  on SDI, 81–82
  secret initiative of, 140–141
  on Shultz, 186
  on Star Wars, 159
  summit preparation by, 97, 119
  on US-Soviet relations, 221
Policy Support Group, 97
Political Bureau (Politburo), 44–47, 51, 106, 144, 209–215
political will, 12
Pompeo, Mike, 260
Prague, 230, 231
*Pravda*, 207
president of the United States, 15, 19
press freedom, 158
public opinion, 126, 169–172, 203, 215, 218
Pugwash conferences, 79
Putin, Vladimir, 259, 276–280

## Q

Quilès, Paul, 254–255

## R

Radio Moscow, 207
Rather, Dan, 115
Reagan, John, 29–30
Reagan, Nancy, 22, 27, 34, 61, 115, 166
Reagan, Nelle, 29–30
Reagan, Ronald, 19
  administration of, 25–29
  anti-Communist leanings of, 32, 36
  Daniloff Affair and, 91
  on democracy, 157
  disappointment of, over summit, 181
  early life of, 29–31
  at Geneva Summit, 55–65
  on Gorbachev, 49
  as governor of California, 32–33
  Hollywood career of, 31–32, 60–61
  inauguration of, 22–23, 271–273
  Moscow summit for, 222
  popularity of, 85
  post-summit, 190–191, 218–223
  post-summit speech by, 197–203
  preparations for Reykjavík Summit and, 98–106
  presidency of, 21–25
  presidential aspirations of, 33–35
  presidential campaign of, 35–36
  private life of, 36–38
  public opinion and, 169–172
  reelection of, 22
  at Reykjavik Summit, 20, 117–120, 122–139, 148–173
  SDI program and, 9, 73–82, 113, 131–132, 134–138, 154–156, 161, 163, 168–169, 174–176, 190, 199–201, 226–227, 273–274

Tibbetts, Paul, 266
Titan II, 14, 16
Truman, Harry, 201
Trump, Donald, 259–260, 276–280
Turkey, 275

**U**
Ukraine, 223
underground bases, 13–20
United Kingdom, 72, 109, 137, 151, 205–206, 275
United Nations, 238, 256
United States
  Germany and, 72–73
  Gorbachev and, 47–49
  gun debate in, 258
  internal situation in, 110–111
  military spending of, 11, 248–251
  preparations for Reykjavík Summit by, 91–106
  public opinion in, 215, 218
  Soviet view of, 213, 216
uranium, 237, 241
US Air Force, 16
US foreign policy, 36, 99–100
US Information Agency, 205
US-Russia relations, 7–8, 260–261
US-Soviet relations, 93–95, 99–100, 126, 221

**V**
Vance, Cyrus, 212
Védrine, Hubert, 47

Velikhov, Evgeny, 176
Velvet Revolution, 231
verification system, 10, 127, 131, 189
Vessey, Jack, 124
Vietnam, 60
Vietnam War, 33, 34, 68
Vorontsov, Yuli, 107

**W**
*Wargames*, 17
Warsaw Pact, 68
Washington, DC, 21
*The Washington Post*, 115
Watergate scandal, 33, 35
Weinberger, Caspar, 28, 101, 140–141
Weinstein, Jack, 246
Werth, Nicolas, 45–46
West Germany, 20, 67, 72, 150–151
White House Working Group, 97
Wick, Charles, 101
World War II, 42–43, 60, 72
Wynam, Jane, 32

**Y**
Yeltsin, Boris, 210

**Z**
Zaikov, Lev, 108, 110
Zakharov, Gennady, 89–90, 91
Zimyanin, Mikhail, 213